First World War
and Army of Occupation
War Diary
France, Belgium and Germany

38 DIVISION
115 Infantry Brigade
South Wales Borderers
11th Battalion
3 December 1915 - 31 January 1918

WO95/2562/2

The Naval & Military Press Ltd
www.nmarchive.com
Published in association with The National Archives

Published by

The Naval & Military Press Ltd

Unit 10 Ridgewood Industrial Park,

Uckfield, East Sussex,

TN22 5QE England

Tel: +44 (0) 1825 749494

www.naval-military-press.com

www.nmarchive.com

This diary has been reprinted in facsimile from the original. Any imperfections are inevitably reproduced and the quality may fall short of modern type and cartographic standards.

© **Crown Copyright**
Images reproduced by permission of The National Archives, London, England, 2015.

Contents

Document type	Place/Title	Date From	Date To
Heading	WO 2562/2 11 Bn Sth Wales Bdrs 1915 Dec-1918 Jan		
Heading	38th Division 115th Infy Bde 11th Bn Sth Wales Bordrs Dec 1915-Jan 1918 Disbanded		
War Diary	Winchester	03/12/1915	03/12/1915
War Diary	Havre	04/12/1915	05/12/1915
War Diary	Aire	06/12/1915	06/12/1915
War Diary	Witternesse	07/12/1915	20/12/1915
War Diary	Riez Du Vinage	21/12/1915	31/12/1915
War Diary	Riez Du Vinage & Richebourg Trench Area	01/01/1916	04/01/1916
War Diary	Riez Du Vinage	05/01/1916	15/01/1916
War Diary	Pont Du Hem	16/01/1916	16/01/1916
War Diary	Winchester HQ. Trenches	17/01/1916	18/01/1916
War Diary	Pont Du Hem	19/01/1916	19/01/1916
War Diary	Winchester HQ. Trenches	20/01/1916	22/01/1916
War Diary	Pont Du Hem	23/01/1916	23/01/1916
War Diary	Les Lobes	24/01/1916	31/01/1916
War Diary	Neuve Chapelle	01/02/1916	04/02/1916
War Diary	Croix Barbee	05/02/1916	08/02/1916
War Diary	Neuve Chapelle	09/02/1916	12/02/1916
War Diary	Croix Barbee	13/02/1916	15/02/1916
War Diary	Le Touret	16/02/1916	19/02/1916
War Diary	Festubert Trenches	20/02/1916	23/02/1916
War Diary	Le Touret	24/02/1916	27/02/1916
War Diary	Festubert Trenches	28/02/1916	29/02/1916
Miscellaneous	From:- O.C 11th Batt S WB (2nd Gwent) To:-Officer 1/4 Infantry Section No. 1 New Armies 3rd Ech G.H.Q B.E.F. Herewith War Diary 11th Batt South Wales Borderes (2nd Gwent) For Month of March	03/04/1916	03/04/1916
War Diary	Festubert Trenches	01/03/1916	01/03/1916
War Diary	Rue De L'Epinette	02/03/1916	05/03/1916
War Diary	Festubert Trenches	06/03/1916	07/03/1916
Heading	11 S W Borders Vol 2 Dec 15 Jan 18		
War Diary	Festubert Trenches	08/03/1916	09/03/1916
War Diary	Le Touret	10/03/1916	13/03/1916
War Diary	Festubert Trenches	14/03/1916	16/03/1916
War Diary	La Pannerie	17/03/1916	23/03/1916
War Diary	Givenchy	24/03/1916	27/03/1916
War Diary	Trenches	28/03/1916	28/03/1916
War Diary	Givenchy Trenches	29/03/1916	31/03/1916
Miscellaneous	D.A.G. 3rd Ech G.H.Q. Attached War Diary 11th Batt South Wales Borderers for April	03/05/1916	03/05/1916
War Diary	Givenchy	01/04/1916	01/04/1916
War Diary	Gorre	02/04/1916	05/04/1916
War Diary	Givenchy	06/04/1916	09/04/1916
War Diary	La Pannerie	10/04/1916	14/04/1916
War Diary	Laventie	15/04/1916	18/04/1916
War Diary	Fauquissart	19/04/1916	22/04/1916
War Diary	Laventie	23/04/1916	26/04/1916
War Diary	Fauquisart	27/04/1916	30/04/1916

Miscellaneous	11th Batt. S.W B (2nd Guest) Herewith War Diary Of 11th Batt S.W.B (2nd Guest) For Month Of May 1916		03/06/1916	03/06/1916
War Diary	Fauquissart		01/05/1916	01/05/1916
War Diary	La Gorgue		02/05/1916	08/05/1916
War Diary	Pont-du-hem		09/05/1916	25/05/1916
War Diary	La Gorgue		26/05/1916	05/06/1916
War Diary	Laventie		06/06/1916	14/06/1916
War Diary	Auchel		15/06/1916	15/06/1916
War Diary	Tincques		16/06/1916	26/06/1916
War Diary	Fortel		27/06/1916	27/06/1916
War Diary	Gezincourt		28/06/1916	30/06/1916
Heading	115th Inf. Bde. 38th Div. War Diary 11th Battn. The South Wales Borderers. July 1916			
War Diary	Toutencourt		01/07/1916	01/07/1916
War Diary	Acheux		02/07/1916	03/07/1916
War Diary	Bure Sur L'ancre		04/07/1916	05/07/1916
War Diary	Carnoy		06/07/1916	14/07/1916
War Diary	Hebuterne		15/07/1916	18/07/1916
War Diary	Courcelles		19/07/1916	22/07/1916
War Diary	Hebuterne		23/07/1916	26/07/1916
War Diary	Courcelles		27/07/1916	28/07/1916
War Diary	Vauchelles		29/07/1916	30/07/1916
War Diary	St Omer		31/07/1916	31/07/1916
War Diary	Millain		01/08/1916	03/08/1916
War Diary	Bollezeele		04/08/1916	23/08/1916
War Diary	Canal Bank		24/08/1916	31/08/1916
War Diary	Front Line		01/09/1916	01/09/1916
War Diary	Canal Bank		02/09/1916	04/09/1916
War Diary	Front Line		05/09/1916	06/09/1916
War Diary	Canal Bank		07/09/1916	10/09/1916
War Diary	Front Line		11/09/1916	14/09/1916
War Diary	Canal Bank		15/09/1916	20/09/1916
War Diary	Camp E		21/09/1916	03/10/1916
War Diary	Front Line		04/10/1916	08/10/1916
War Diary	Canal Bank		09/10/1916	11/10/1916
War Diary	Front Line		12/10/1916	15/10/1916
War Diary	Canal Bank		16/10/1916	20/10/1916
War Diary	Front Line		21/10/1916	25/10/1916
War Diary	Camp P		26/10/1916	04/11/1916
War Diary	Front Line		05/11/1916	09/11/1916
War Diary	Canal Bank		09/11/1916	15/11/1916
War Diary	Front Line		15/11/1916	19/11/1916
War Diary	Canal Bank		20/11/1916	23/11/1916
War Diary	Front Line		24/11/1916	30/11/1916
War Diary	Divisional Reserve		01/12/1916	03/12/1916
War Diary	Support Right Subsector.		04/12/1916	12/12/1916
War Diary	Elverdinghe Defences		13/12/1916	17/12/1916
War Diary	Roussel Farm.		18/12/1916	22/12/1916
War Diary	Tatinghem		23/12/1916	21/01/1917
War Diary	G. Camp.		21/01/1917	22/01/1917
War Diary	Roussel Farm		23/01/1917	28/01/1917
War Diary	Baesinghe Chateau		28/01/1917	31/01/1917
War Diary	Baesinghe		01/02/1917	02/02/1917
War Diary	Roussel Farm		03/02/1917	10/02/1917
War Diary	Front Line		11/02/1917	14/02/1917
War Diary	Roussel Farm		15/02/1917	22/02/1917

Type	Location	Start	End
War Diary	Front Line	23/02/1917	26/02/1917
War Diary	X Camp	27/02/1917	02/03/1917
War Diary	Machine Gun Farm	03/03/1917	18/03/1917
War Diary	Bleuet Farm	19/03/1917	22/03/1917
War Diary	Front Line	23/03/1917	26/03/1917
War Diary	Bleuet Farm	27/03/1917	31/03/1917
War Diary	Frontline	31/03/1917	31/03/1917
War Diary	Boesinghe Sector	02/04/1917	03/04/1917
War Diary	Bleuet. Farm.	04/04/1917	07/04/1917
War Diary	Boesinghe Sector	08/04/1917	13/04/1917
War Diary	Bleuet Farm	14/04/1917	19/04/1917
War Diary	Machine Gun Farm	21/04/1917	30/04/1917
Operation(al) Order(s)	Battalion Orders No 15. By Lieut Colonel A.H. Radice. Commanding 11th Service Battalion South Wales Borderers. (2nd Gwent.)	13/04/1917	13/04/1917
Operation(al) Order(s)	Battalion Orders No 16. By Major E.J. De. P. O'Kelly. Commanding 11th Service Battalion South Wales Borderers. (2nd Gwent)	18/04/1917	18/04/1917
War Diary	Elverdinghe	01/05/1917	01/05/1917
War Diary	Bollezeele	06/05/1917	16/05/1917
War Diary	Houtkerque	18/05/1917	18/05/1917
War Diary	M. Camp.	19/05/1917	19/05/1917
War Diary	Bleuet Farm.	24/05/1917	24/05/1917
War Diary	Boesinghe	25/05/1917	01/06/1917
War Diary	Support Battn Area	02/06/1917	02/06/1917
War Diary	Boesinghe Sector.	02/06/1917	06/06/1917
War Diary	Front Line	06/06/1917	06/06/1917
War Diary	Boesinghe Sector.	10/06/1917	12/06/1917
War Diary	Cardouen Fm.	13/06/1917	13/06/1917
War Diary	Proven	14/06/1917	28/06/1917
War Diary	Westrehem	01/07/1917	16/07/1917
War Diary	Guarbecque	16/07/1917	17/07/1917
War Diary	Pradelles	17/07/1917	18/07/1917
War Diary	Steenvorde	18/07/1917	19/07/1917
War Diary	Proven	19/07/1917	20/07/1917
War Diary	Proven Area.	20/07/1917	20/07/1917
War Diary	St. Sixte Area.	21/07/1917	29/07/1917
War Diary	Dublin Camp.	30/07/1917	31/07/1917
War Diary	Canal Bank	31/07/1917	31/07/1917
War Diary	Green Line	31/07/1917	31/07/1917
War Diary	Steenbeck	31/07/1917	31/07/1917
War Diary	Steenbeck U28a62 To U28d3.3	01/08/1917	02/08/1917
War Diary	Mauser Cot C.14a 5.9	02/08/1917	02/08/1917
War Diary	Support Area	02/08/1917	02/08/1917
War Diary	E. Canal Bank. N. of Swaanhoff Fm. C.13b 5.3	03/08/1917	03/08/1917
War Diary	Canal Bank	03/08/1917	05/08/1917
War Diary	Elverdinghe	05/08/1917	05/08/1917
War Diary	St. Sixte	05/08/1917	05/08/1917
War Diary	Staines	06/08/1917	18/08/1917
War Diary	Canal Bank	18/08/1917	23/08/1917
War Diary	Line. U29a 8.6	23/08/1917	30/08/1917
War Diary	B23c44	30/08/1917	31/08/1917
War Diary	Malakoff Farm Area	01/09/1917	04/09/1917
War Diary	Proven Area	10/09/1917	11/09/1917
War Diary	Eecke Area	12/09/1917	12/09/1917
War Diary	Morbecque Area	13/09/1917	13/09/1917

War Diary	Estaires Area	14/09/1917	15/09/1917
War Diary	Talana Farm	15/09/1917	15/09/1917
War Diary	Talana Farm	05/09/1917	09/09/1917
War Diary	Armentieres Sector	09/09/1917	09/09/1917
War Diary	Armentieres Sector.	16/09/1917	22/09/1917
War Diary	L'Epinette Sub-Sector.	23/09/1917	27/09/1917
War Diary	Armentieres Sector.	28/09/1917	30/09/1917
War Diary	L'Epinette	01/10/1917	02/10/1917
War Diary	Laundries H5A 5.7 Sheet 36	03/10/1917	08/10/1917
War Diary	L'Epinette Sub-Sector Armentieres Section	09/10/1917	17/10/1917
War Diary	Laundries H5a 5.7	18/10/1917	20/10/1917
War Diary	Laundries H5a 5.7 Sheet 36	21/10/1917	26/10/1917
War Diary	L'Epinette Sub Sector Armentieres Section	27/10/1917	04/11/1917
War Diary	Laundries H 5 A 5.7	05/11/1917	16/11/1917
War Diary	L'Epinette Sub Sector Armentieres Section	17/11/1917	22/11/1917
War Diary	Subsidiary Line	23/11/1917	23/11/1917
War Diary	Armentieres Section	23/11/1917	26/11/1917
War Diary	Subsidiary Line Armentieres Section	27/11/1917	28/11/1917
War Diary	L'Epinette Sub-Sector. Armentieres. Section	29/11/1917	04/12/1917
War Diary	Laundries H5a 5.7	05/12/1917	10/12/1917
War Diary	L'Epinette Sub-Sector Armentieres Section	10/12/1917	17/12/1917
War Diary	Armentieres Sector	18/12/1917	18/12/1917
War Diary	Sailly Sur La Lys	19/12/1917	12/01/1918
War Diary	Estaires Area (South)	13/01/1918	31/01/1918

WO 2562/2

11 BN STH WALES BDRS
1915 DEC - 1918 JAN

38TH DIVISION
115TH INFY BDE.

11TH BN STH WALES BORDRS
DEC 1915-JAN 1918

DISBANDED

Army Form C. 2118

WAR DIARY
or
INTELLIGENCE SUMMARY
(Erase heading not required.)

Instructions regarding War Diaries and Intelligence Summaries are contained in F.S. Regs., Part II. and the Staff Manual respectively. Title Pages will be prepared in manuscript.

115/38

Place	Date	Hour	Summary of Events and Information	Remarks and references to Appendices
Winchester	1915 Dec 3	7.30 a.m.	Batn. left HAZELY DOWN Camp by march route for SOUTHAMPTON	
		7-8 p.m.	Embarked on two transports from SOUTHAMPTON	
HAVRE	Dec 4	7.0 a.m.	Batn. disembarked & proceeded to rest camp for night	
HAVRE	Dec 5	9.0 a.m.	Batn. proceeded to Ry. station by route march	
		12 noon	Train left	
		6 p.m.	Halt for Tea	
AIRE	Dec 6	9.0 a.m.	Arrived AIRE and proceeded by route march to WITTERNESSE being accommodated in billets	
WITTERNESSE	Dec 7 to Dec 13		Battalion Training	
"	Dec 14-19	11.0 a.m.	Batn. lined road as Guard of Honour to General French	
"	Dec 20	7.50 a.m.	Batn. proceeded by route march to RIEZ DU VINAGE	
RIEZ DU VINAGE	Dec 21 to Dec 27		Batn. Training	

WAR DIARY or INTELLIGENCE SUMMARY

(Erase heading not required.)

Place	Date	Hour	Summary of Events and Information	Remarks and references to Appendices
RIEZ DU VINAGE	1915 Dec 28	8.45 a.m	Batn. proceeded by motor bus to be attached for instruction in the trenches in the RICHEBOURG area. Companies being attached to units as follows:— A. Coy. to 7th R. Lancs. B. Coy to 7th E. Lancs. C. Coy to 7th S. Lancs D. Coy to 7th L. Lancs. H.Q to 7th E. Lancs.	
	Dec 29 to Dec 31st		Companies in the Trenches. Details returned at RIEZ DU VINAGE	

Army Form C. 2118

WAR DIARY
or
INTELLIGENCE SUMMARY

(Erase heading not required.)

Instructions regarding War Diaries and Intelligence Summaries are contained in F.S. Regs., Part II. and the Staff Manual respectively. Title Pages will be prepared in manuscript.

Place	Date 1916	Hour	Summary of Events and Information	Remarks and references to Appendices
RIEZ DU VINAGE + RICHEBOURG Trench area G	Jan 1st – Jan 5th		Companies in the line. Details left behind at RIEZ continued their training. The following casualties were sustained. 22146 Pte. Cripps. 21714 Pte Cox. 2700 Pte. Pitt. 22089 Pte. Barrett. All wounded.	
RIEZ DU VINAGE	Jan 5th – Jan 11th		Battalion concentrated at RICHEBOURG and marched back to RIEZ DU VINAGE.	
RIEZ DU VINAGE	Jan 6th – Jan 14th		Battalion Training.	
RIEZ DU VINAGE	Jan 15th		Battalion proceed into billets by march route at PONT DU HEM.	
PONT DU HEM	Jan 16		Battalion took over Trenches from 10th S.W.B. with H.Q WINCHESTER HO. Rifle & machine gun fire active all night. Following casualty sustained. 11972 Pte Barry Wounded.	

Army Form C. 2118

WAR DIARY
or
INTELLIGENCE SUMMARY

(Erase heading not required.)

Instructions regarding War Diaries and Intelligence Summaries are contained in F. S. Regs., Part II. and the Staff Manual respectively. Title Pages will be prepared in manuscript.

Place	Date 1916	Hour	Summary of Events and Information	Remarks and references to Appendices
WINCHESTER H.Q. Trenches	Jan 17	12 noon	Batn H.Q shelled 14 shells	
		3 pm	" " " 8 shells	
			Casualties 11/22564 Pte Colignon wounded (since died)	
			" 11/2004 2 Pte Davis "	
"	Jan 18	1.30 p.m	French Post & Winchester H.Q. shelled	
		6.0 pm	Batn moved into Reserve at PONT DU HEM.	
			Casualties 11/21677 Pte Price ? wounded	
			11/22319 " Gibbs ? e "	
PONT DU HEM.	Jan 19		Billets in reserve	
WINCHESTER H.Q. Trenches	Jan 20		Casualties 11/21589 Pte Thomas W. wounded	
			11/15364 Sergt Whiting " "	
"	Jan 21st		Trenches	
"	Jan 22nd		Batn relieved out of Trenches & returned to PONT DU HEM.	
			Casualties 11/2169 Cpl Pointer wounded 11/22505 Pte Porter 11/21884 Pte Jones ? wounded	
			11/22579 Pte Jones 11/22616 " "	

Army Form C. 2118

WAR DIARY
or
INTELLIGENCE SUMMARY

(Erase heading not required.)

Instructions regarding War Diaries and Intelligence Summaries are contained in F.S. Regs., Part II. and the Staff Manual respectively. Title Pages will be prepared in manuscript.

Place	Date 1916	Hour	Summary of Events and Information	Remarks and references to Appendices
PONT DU HEM	Jan 23		Moved from PONT DU HEM into billets and LOCON.	
LES LOBES	Jan 24 to Jan 30th		Battalion Training &c.	
LES LOBES	Jan 31		Battalion moved by route march via RICHEBOURG to trenches at NEUVE CHAPELLE. Relief complete 9.10 pm	
NEUVE CHAPELLE				

Army Form C. 2118

WAR DIARY
or
INTELLIGENCE SUMMARY
(Erase heading not required.)

Instructions regarding War Diaries and Intelligence Summaries are contained in F.S. Regs., Part II. and the Staff Manual respectively. Title Pages will be prepared in manuscript.

Place	Date 1916	Hour	Summary of Events and Information	Remarks and references to Appendices
NEUVE CHAPELLE	Feb 1st		Trenches.	
"	Feb 2nd		Trenches. Casualties. 2nd Lieut S.G. Hutton Halcott. 11/21697 Pte Morris. 11/21764 Pte Davies. 11/22211 Pte Baker all wounded.	
"	Feb 3		Trenches. Casualties. 11/21893 Pte Bechlington. 11/21787 Pte Gates. 11/22013 Pte Sleepour all wounded.	
"	Feb 4		Trenches. Relieved by 10th S.W.B. Casualties. 11/22176 Pte Group 11/15201 Serj. Freeberg	
			To reserve billets at CROIX BARBÉE	
CROIX BARBÉE	Feb 5		Reserve billets	
"	" 6		"	
"	" 7		2nd Lieut T.H. Davis joined. 11/21665 Pte Evans killed.	
"	" 8		Relieved 10th S.W.B. in Trenches at NEUVE CHAPELLE	

WAR DIARY or INTELLIGENCE SUMMARY

Army Form C. 2118

Place	Date 1916	Hour	Summary of Events and Information	Remarks and references to Appendices
NEUVE CHAPELLE	Feb 9th		Trenches. Right Coy 'D' shelled. Casualties. 11/21640 Sergt Harris killed. 11/21631 Pte Stock. 11/22333 Pte Evans. 11/22 44 Comm Sergt Durrer all wounded.	
"	Feb 10th		Trenches. Right Coy 'D' Shelled. Enemy used stops of our guns & 60 lb Trench Mortars. Casualties. 11/22613 Pte Stead. 11/22634 Pte Sullivan. 11/22261 Pte Reece. 11/22403 Pte Morgan. 11/21510 Pte Hobson wounded. 2 Lieuts E.B. Barker and E.H. Griffiths joined.	
"	Feb 11th		Trenches. 2 Lieut R.E. Carrington joined.	
"	Feb 12th		Trenches. Relieved by 10th S.W.B. and returned to CROIX BARBÉE	
CROIX BARBÉE	Feb 13		Reserve billets. A Coy. to MOGG'S HOLE and EUSTON CORNER POSTS	

Army Form C. 2118

WAR DIARY
or
INTELLIGENCE SUMMARY
(Erase heading not required.)

Instructions regarding War Diaries and Intelligence Summaries are contained in F.S. Regs., Part II. and the Staff Manual respectively. Title Pages will be prepared in manuscript.

Place	Date	Hour	Summary of Events and Information	Remarks and references to Appendices
CROIX BARBEE	Feb 14		Reserve Billets. 2 Lieut R.M. HEPPELL and 60 ranks joined.	
"	Feb 15		Battalion moved by march route to LE TOURET and went into Bat'n reserve to the 56th Brigade. Reserve billets.	
LE TOURET	Feb 16		"	
"	" 17		"	
"	" 18		"	
"	" 19		Batt'n to Trenches via Rue Du Bois Rue Epinette to islands at FESTUBERT. Relieving 13th Essex Reg.t	
FESTUBERT Trenches	" 20 "		Casualties Cap.t S. Cullimore killed. 11/22052 P.te Jones. 11/21950 P.te Hochmeyer 11/22163 L/c Gardner wounded. 11/21942 P.te Hughes wounded. 11/22165 P.te Fus. (Bandsman) attached for instruction. One Coy. 10th Lanc Fus. attached for instruction.	

WAR DIARY
or
INTELLIGENCE SUMMARY
(Erase heading not required.)

Army Form C. 2118

Instructions regarding War Diaries and Intelligence Summaries are contained in F.S. Regs., Part II. and the Staff Manual respectively. Title Pages will be prepared in manuscript.

Place	Date 1916	Hour	Summary of Events and Information	Remarks and references to Appendices
Festubert Trenches	Feb 21st		Trenches.	
"	Feb 22		Trenches.	
"	Feb 23		Trenches. Relieved by 10th S.W.B. Batn. to reserve at LE TOURET.	
LE TOURET	Feb 24		Reserve Billets.	
	25		"	
	26		To Trenches FESTUBERT in relief of 10th S.W.B.	
	27		10th Leuc. Fus. marched off on completion of instruction. 11th Gloucesters (Bantams) attached for instruction.	
Festubert Trenches	28		Trenches	
	29		Trenches Casualties 1/225 40 Pte Blackwell wounded.	

11/A563

From :- O.C 11th Batt S.W.B (2nd Gwent)

To :- Officer i/c
        Infantry Section
        No 1 New Armies
        3rd Ech G.H.Q
        B.E.F

Herewith War Diary 11th Batt South Wales Borderers (2nd Gwent) for month of March.

               J.P. Hamer
               Lieut & Adjutant

        11th Batt S.W.B (2nd Gwent)

3/4/16

11th Batt South Wales Borderers (2nd Gwent)

WAR DIARY or INTELLIGENCE SUMMARY

Army Form C. 2118

Place	Date	Hour	Summary of Events and Information	Remarks and references to Appendices
Festubert Trenches	July 1 1916		Casualties. 21630 Sergt. White, 32540 Pr. Blackwell, 32493 Pr. Williams (wounded)	
Rue de l'Epinette	July 2		Left trenches for support billets at Rue de l'Epinette. Relieved by 10 S.W.B. 5.30 P.M. Casualties. 22511 Pr. Jones, 21720 " Riley wounded do	
"	July 3		Bathed at Letouret	
"	July 4		Rue de l'Epinette Shelled between 11 AM and 12 noon. Lt. Col Gausen assumed temp command of Brigade.	
"	July 5		Bath.	
Festubert Trenches	July 6		Bat. proceeded to trenches, relieving 10th S.W.B.	
"	July 7		14th Bat Gloucester Regt attacked, relieved by Sherwood Foresters (15th Bn.) During night flag in no man's land S.28.A.2.5 brought in by D Coy. Henry O.P Shelled in morning. Casualties. 33263 Pr. Smith wounded	

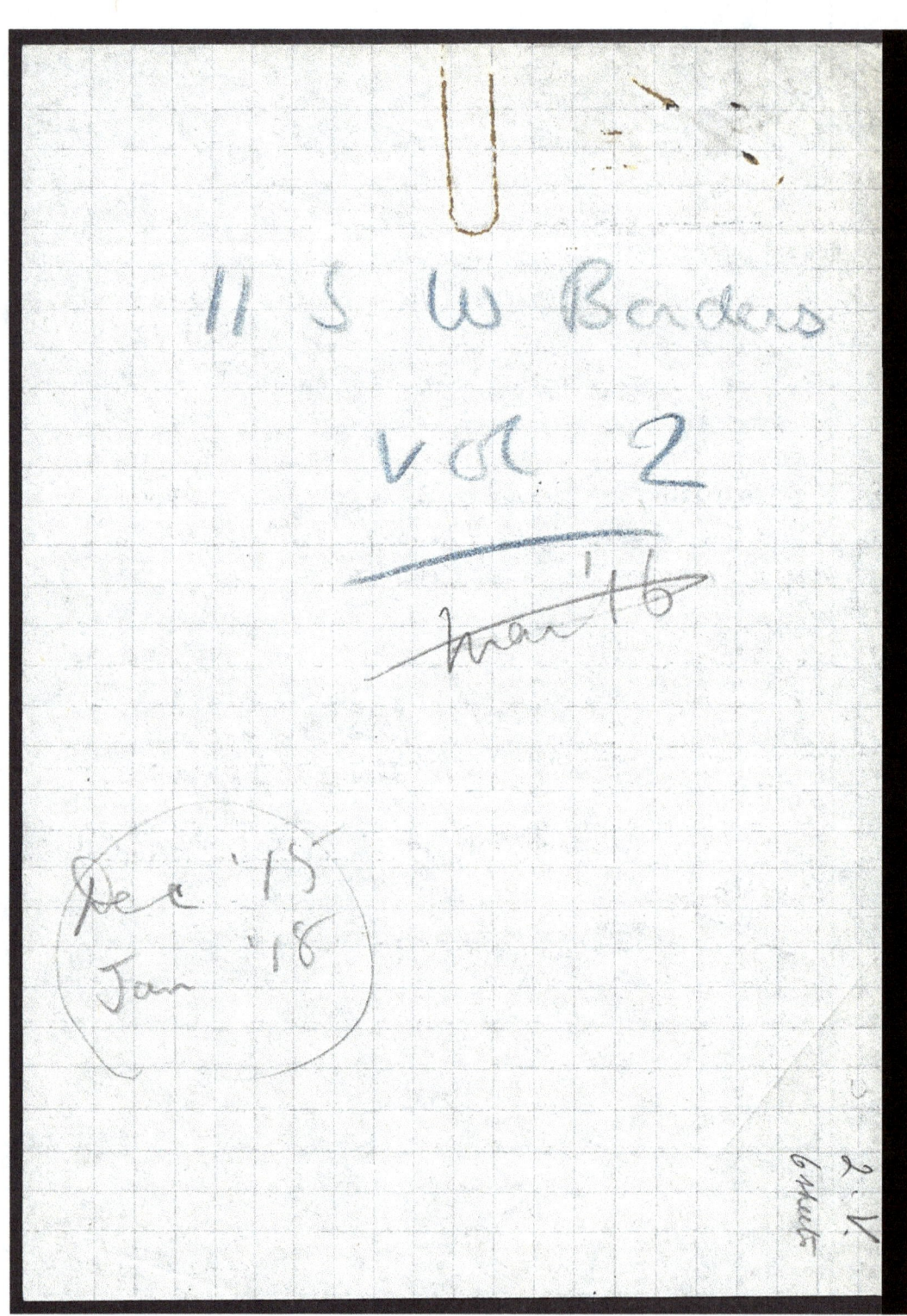

Army Form C. 2118

11th Batt S.W.B (2nd Lieut)

WAR DIARY
or
INTELLIGENCE SUMMARY
(Erase heading not required.)

Place	Date 1916	Hour	Summary of Events and Information	Remarks and references to Appendices
Festubert Trenches	Mch 8th		Trenches. Quiet day.	
"	9th		Capt L.R. Lewis admitted to 130th F.A. Casualties. 22595 Pte Cornick. Wounded.	
Festubert	10th		Relieved by 10th SWB returned to reserve Billet at Lebourse X Roads	
"	Mch 11th		Wire defence of reserve line improved	
"	Mch 12th		worked on wire	
"	13		worked on wire	
Festubert Trenches	" 14th		Trenches. Relieved 10th SWB. Lt.Col Gaussen resumed Command.	
"	" 15		Trenches. Casualties. 22529 Pte Stephen. Killed. 22537 Cpl Davis. Wounded. 2nd Lt Summers joined the Batt. 2nd Lt Taylor	

Army Form C. 2118

11th Batt SWB (2nd quet)

WAR DIARY
or
INTELLIGENCE SUMMARY
(Erase heading not required.)

Instructions regarding War Diaries and Intelligence Summaries are contained in F.S. Regs., Part II. and the Staff Manual respectively. Title Pages will be prepared in manuscript.

Place	Date	Hour	Summary of Events and Information	Remarks and references to Appendices
Festubert Zenekes	Oct 16 1915		Zenekes. Relieved by 14th RWF, & proceeded to La Pannerie for Brigade rest. Casualties Capt. R.J. Evans Wounded.	
La Pannerie	" 17		Rest Billets. 20 men attached to 123rd Fus. Co.	
"	" 18		Furnished working party of 400 men for work on wire at Festubert. Capt. Ormsby Johnson inspected Paybook (A.B 64)	
"	" 19 Sunday		Church parade in morning	
"	" 20		Training in bombing & Sniping	
"	" 21		Inspection of troops Billets by the Brigadier. Casualties 21744 Pte. Keary at. 123rd R.E. Wounded. Bath. Locon.	
"	" 22		2nd Lt. R.C. Carrington & 40 men to 19th Pioneer Batt. Permanent mining fatigue.	

11th Batt S.W.B (2 Lieut)

WAR DIARY
or
INTELLIGENCE SUMMARY
(Erase heading not required.)

Army Form C. 2118

Place	Date	Hour	Summary of Events and Information	Remarks and references to Appendices
La Pannerie	1916 Mch 23		Baths. Recon. Bombing & Sniping practice.	
Givenchy	24		Batt marched to Givenchy took over support in Village line from 1st Batt R.W.F.	
			Lt Col Gaussen assumed command of Brigade.	
			2nd Lt. Appn Jones Batt.	
	25		Support trench. Furnishes fatigue and working parties for work in Jap. communication trench. Village line. D Coy in Givenchy Keep.	
	26		" Fatigues	
	27		" Fatigues	
	28		Batt took over front line (left sector) from 10th SWB. relief complete 11.45 PM	
			Casualties Lt. J.H.C. Griffith accidentally wounded	
Guinchy			Hannemaym demonstration near Essars	

11th Batt N.F. (2nd equel)

Army Form C. 2118

WAR DIARY
or
INTELLIGENCE SUMMARY
(Erase heading not required.)

Place	Date 1918	Hour	Summary of Events and Information	Remarks and references to Appendices
Gouzeaucourt Trenches	Mch 29		Trenches. Casualties 21525 Pte Green. wounded.	
"	30		Trenches. 2/Lt Summers admitted 129th F.A. 2/Lt Heppel " " Casualties. 21506 Pte Davies wounded.	
"	31		Trenches. Casualties D19940 Pte Hodges. J. Killed	

D A G
2nd Ech
G H Q

Attached War diary
11th Batt South Wales
Borderers for April

3/5/16

T.P.Hamer
Lieut a A/y
11th Batt S W B

WAR DIARY or INTELLIGENCE SUMMARY

Army Form C. 2118

11th Batt. S.W.B. (2nd Gwent)

Vol 3 / Ap 16

Place	Date	Hour	Summary of Events and Information	Remarks and references to Appendices
Givenchy	April 1		Trenches. Casualties. Capt. L.C.W. Williams Wounded. (Self Shot) Pres. Keen, Roberts & Barry Wounded	
"	2		Reserve Billets. Relieved by 10th S.W.B. at 4.45 pm	
"	3		"	
"	4		" Lt. Col. Gawen resumed Command.	
"	5		" In the evening relieved 10th S.W.B. in Front Line.	
Givenchy	6		Trenches. Casualties. Pte. Underwood Cpl. Brown Sgt. Cronin Pte. Simmonds } Wounded.	
"	7		Trenches. Small defensive mine exploded by 123rd R.E. at 8 pm.	
"	8		do. Casualties. Sgt. Evans Pte. Woodford } Wounded.	

WAR DIARY or INTELLIGENCE SUMMARY

Army Form C. 2118

11th Batt S WB (2nd Gwent)

(Erase heading not required.)

Place	Date	Hour	Summary of Events and Information	Remarks and references to Appendices
Givenchy	April 9		Trenches. Relieved by 15th RWF at 3.30 p.m. marched to Beguinage at La Gorgue.	
La Gorgue	10		Billets.	
"	11		do. Bath.	
"	12		do. 460 men went in Motor Buses to Le Jonet for wiring Chinese etc.	
"	13		do. Bath.	
"	14		Batt left La Gorgue at 9 a.m. marched to Estaires, when Batt billeted for the night previous to marching on to Laventie.	
"	15		Marched to Laventie. Relieved the Durham Light Infantry in reserve. 'B' Coy in Rugs also 1 platoon 'C' Coy	
Laventie	16		Reserve Billets. Working parties for communication trench [fontline]	
"	17		" " " " "	

WAR DIARY 11th Batt S W B (2nd Queens)
or
INTELLIGENCE SUMMARY

Army Form C. 2118

(Erase heading not required.)

Place	Date	Hour	Summary of Events and Information	Remarks and references to Appendices
Laventie	April 18		Reserve billets. Working parties.	
Fauquissart	19		Trenches. Relieved 10th Bat SWB. Autichamps on our left. 16th Welsh on right.	
"	20		do. Lt. Col. Gawen assumes command of 115th Brigade. Casualties. Sergt Lewis wounded.	
"	21		do. A draft of 21 O.R. arrives from base. 2/Lieut. Palmer and 2/Lieut. Salathiel reports for duty.	
"	22		do. Casualties. Pte Challoner wounded.	
Laventie	23		Bat. was relieved by 10th SWB. returns to reserve billets at Laventie. Major D Grant Dalton left to assume command of 19 Welsh Regt. Capt. A Dawes assumed Command.	
do	24		Billets. "B" Coy in Reps.	

WAR DIARY
INTELLIGENCE SUMMARY

1st Batt S.W.B (2nd Queens)

Army Form C. 2118

Place	Date	Hour	Summary of Events and Information	Remarks and references to Appendices
Laventie	April 25		"B" Coy in Trps.	
"	26		do	
"	27		Relieved 16th SWB at 10 p.m.	
"	28		Heavy bombardment of front line. Communication trench by Enemy. Casualties. 2 Lieut W.J. Watts wounded. Pte Gearn wounded. Pte Dobson wounded. Pte Phillips killed.	
"	29		Casualties. L/Cpl Saunders wounded. Pte Dun Jones wounded. Pte William wounded.	
"	30		Ammunition & Bomb Store at Gravelin Keep struck by trench shell. Causing trouble of the building & ammunition to take refuge by fire. Casualties Pte Philli wounded.	J. Mann Lt Col

11th Batt S.W.B (2nd Gwent)

Herewith War Diary of
11th Batt S.W.B (2nd Gwent)
for month of May 1916

3/6/16

11 S.W.B.
Army /Form C. 2118

Vol 4 May 1916
XXVIII

WAR DIARY
or
INTELLIGENCE SUMMARY
(Erase heading not required)
Summary of Events and Information

11th Batt. South Wales Borderers (2nd Gwent)

Place	Date	Hour		Remarks and references to Appendices
Fauquissart	May 1st		Trenches. Relieved by 13th R.W.F. marched to La Gorgue via Estain.	
La Gorgue	2		Billets. Rest and general clean up.	
do	3		do	
"	4		do ⎫	
"	5		" ⎪	
"	6		" ⎬ Training.	
"	7		" ⎪	
"	8		" ⎭	
"	9		"	
Pont-du-Hem	10		Relieved 15th Batt Welsh Regt in support billets. A Coy in Posts	
do	11		Support billets. Working parties and baths.	
"	12		" " " A Coy relieved by D.C.	Pte Marshall A Coy Casualty (wounded)
"	13		" Draft of 12 men joining. A Coy relieved 10th SWB in Peffreces Mortar Range. D Coy in Traps.	
"	14		Trenches A.B.C in front line. D Coy in Traps.	
"	15		Trenches Casualties	Pte Collins A Coy ⎫ Pte Stone B " ⎬ wounded Pte James C " ⎭
"	16		Trenches Casualties	Pte Rogers B " wounded (accidentally) C Coy in Post
"	17		Support billets. Relieved by 10th SWB.	Pte Peary M Coy Casualty (wounded)
"	18		" Bath. Working parties.	

WAR DIARY or INTELLIGENCE SUMMARY

Army Form C. 2118

(Erase heading not required.)

Place	Date	Hour	Summary of Events and Information	Remarks and references to Appendices
Pont du Jour	May 19		Support billets. Working parties.	
"	20		" " "	
"	21		To the trench "reliene 10" SWB in supports "Moats Grange." Casualties. D Coy in Trenches. Pte Morgan A Coy, Pte Davies B Coy } wounded.	
"	22		Trenches. Our T.M's and Artillery bombarded enemy line + front line with the object of getting a Coy in one Enemy retaliated inflicting 1 Casualty. Pte Fern C Coy, Pte Hubert C Coy, Pte White C Coy } wounded. Pte Siter B Coy, Pte Robins R.S., Pte Boynton B Coy.	
"	23		Trenches. A party 10 SWB attempted a raid on enemy trenches, supports by artillery + T.M's. They arrayed the enemy who promptly retaliate heavily on our front support line Causing several Casualties. Pte Gower B Coy } killed in action. Pte Plummer C Coy. Pte Pattison C Coy. Pte William C Coy. Pte Boone C Coy. Pte Farley C Coy. Pte Gryl C Coy. Pte Powell B Coy. Pte Bassett C Coy. Pte Welford B Coy. Pte Cousin A Coy. Pte Frape A Coy. Pte Dawson B Coy. Pte Clement C Coy. Pte Jones C Coy. Pte Webb B Coy. } wounded	
"	24		Trenches. Pte Russell accidentally shot himself through foot.	
"	25		Relieved by 14th Batt RWF and marched to La Gorgue	
La Gorgue	26		Billets. Rest. Several clean up.	
"	27		" " Orders received to be in readiness to depart a reserve to any party. Coys Cms act to be notified.	

WAR DIARY
or
INTELLIGENCE SUMMARY

Army Form C. 2118

Place	Date	Hour	Summary of Events and Information	Remarks and references to Appendices
La Gorgue	May 28		Bieez. Working parties & Bath. Training.	
"	29		do Working parties. Training.	
"	30		do Went on wire during day. Wire heard on on right. At about 9.40 pm enemy were reported to have commenced "Stand to". At 10 pm Battn marched off to "Bout de Ville" and orders of G.O.C. 35th Div. On arrival at Bout de Ville were reported than enemy, who had attempted an attack on our line near Pierre Chapelle, had be driven back. That all was quiet. Batt then returned to La Gorgue arriving in billets 12.30 midnight.	
"	31		Bieez. In the morning working parties and Gas demonstration at Div Gas School, La Gorgue. Battalion Sports in the afternoon.	

J. Mauer
La. Regt, Lt. 73

WAR DIARY
11th BATT. SOUTH WALES BORDERERS (2nd GWENT)
INTELLIGENCE SUMMARY

XXXVIII 11.S.W.B. June
Vol 2
5.V. 2 sheet

Army Form C. 2118

Place	Date	Hour	Summary of Events and Information	Remarks and references to Appendices
La Gorgue	June 1		Brigade reserve billets. Training.	
"	2		" Route March with 10 Welsh Regt. Major Smith 10 Welsh in command.	
"	3		" Work on La Gorgue defences.	
"	4		" "	
"	5		" Church Parade.	
"	6		March to Laventie, to relieve 13 Welsh Regt. in support. Relieved 2/4 Oxford & Bucks attached for instruction.	
Laventie	7		Support billets. Working parties. Day in Support Billets.	
"	8		" A party of 100 men supplied for work on new level, which was carried out successfully at night, without any casualties.	
"	9		" Baths. 2/4 Royal Berkshire Regt. relieved 2/4 Oxford & Bucks.	
"	10		" Orders to relieve 10 SWB in line cancelled, orders to stand fast.	
"	11		" La Gorgue. Stayed the night, in same billets as we occupied on Brigade Reserve.	
"	12		Marched to La Gorgue.	
"	13		Marched to Calonne sur la Lys.	
			Calonne sur la Lys. Memorial Service to Lord Kitchener.	
"	14		Marched to Auchel. Stayed the night. at 11 P.M. train advanced 60 minutes.	

Army Form C. 2118

WAR DIARY
or
INTELLIGENCE SUMMARY

(Erase heading not required.)

Instructions regarding War Diaries and Intelligence Summaries are contained in F. S. Regs., Part II. and the Staff Manual respectively. Title Pages will be prepared in manuscript.

Place	Date	Hour	Summary of Events and Information	Remarks and references to Appendices
Auchel	June 15		Marched off at 6.15 AM for Jircques (Divisional Training Area).	
Jircques	16		Billet. 700 men supplied for work on practice trench.	
"	17		" Company training on manoeuvre Area.	
"	18		" " " " " "	
"	19		" " " " " "	
"	20		" " " " " "	
"	21		" " " " " "	
"	22		" " " " " "	
"	23		Battalion Field Day.	
"	24		Brigade Field Day.	
"	25		Divisional Field Day.	
"	26		Marched to Fortel arriving 2.30 am.	
Fortel	27		" at 7.15 pm to Sevincourt arriving 1.30 AM.	
Sevincourt	28		Rest.	
"	29		"	
"	30		At 4.30 pm marched off to Toutencourt, arriving 12 midnight.	

J. C. Bauer
Lieut. & Adjt. 11th AIF

115th Inf.Bde.
38th Div.

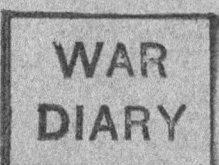

11th BATTN. THE SOUTH WALES BORDERERS.

J U L Y

1 9 1 6

INTELLIGENCE SUMMARY

11th Batt. Suffolk (2nd Event[?])

Place	Date	Hour	Summary of Events and Information	Remarks and references to Appendices
Antoinement Albert	July 1		March to Albert, arrived in Albert 12:30 AM Rested.	
"	2		Marched to Louvencourt, arrived in Halloy 2:15 A.M.	
"	3		Rested.	
Louvencourt	4		Marched to Louvencourt	
"	5			
Louvencourt	6		Marched to Battlefield Wood at 8 PM arriving at 2:30 AM July 7th.	
"	7		Attacked Mametz Wood at 8:24 AM in conjunction with battn. (Brig. 16 Welsh), attack failed. Battalions reformed and made a second attack at about 11 AM, this attack also failed. Casualties killed Lt Homer acty adjt wounded, Capt Monteith, Capt Browning & 2/Lt Lowe 2/Lt Woodcock, 2/Lt Whittaker, 2/Lt Leatheil 2/Lt Covington & 2/Lt Ackerley and 1 2/O.R.	
	8		Relieved by 115th Brigade at 3 AM.	
	9		Resting in Ravenna till 8 AM when D and C Bos went up to Caterpillar Wood and Marlboro Wood and relieved the 10th Welsh 114 Ridge. A & B Bs went to Mametz Wood to reinforce 113th Ridge.	
	10		B & D Bos held Bazentin and Marlboro Wood, and A & B attacked in Mametz Wood & D still in the two woods and were relieved by 8th Devons at 12 PM.	
	11		A & B were relieved in Mametz Wood by two Bos from the 7th Division Casualties 6 ORs killed and 2 (?) 2/Lt Shelly wounded, 2/Lt Futcher, 2/Lt Heal, 2/Lt Rumer & 2/Lt Phipps wounded, 1/Lt Miller, H.B.Browning	

INTELLIGENCE SUMMARY

(Erase heading not required.)

Instructions regarding War Diaries and Intelligence Summaries are contained in F.S. Regs., Part II and the Staff Manual respectively. Title Pages will be prepared in manuscript.

Place	Date	Hour	Summary of Events and Information	Remarks and references to Appendices
Festubert Cauchy	July 12		Bivouac all day, resting	
	13	5 AM	Marched off to Warley-Ballon and then taken by buses to Bavin	
	14	2:45 PM	Marched to trenches & in the Helutiers sector and relieved #11/10 # Gloucesters	
Helutiere	15		trenches	
"	16		trenches	
"	17		trenches	
"	18		trenches and relieved 5 PM by 10# KRRB and marched to Bouzelles	
Bouzelles	19		Billets in Bouzelles Battalion bathed at Bavin	
"	20		Bouzelles billets working parties furnished the front line at night	
"	21		" " " "	
"	22		" " Relieved the 10# KRRB at 5 PM relief complete at 7.30 PM	
Helutiere	23		trenches	
"	24		"	
"	25		"	
"	26		" A to taken by buses to Eyoncourt, B. C. & D. Coys relieved by 10# KRRB at 7.30 PM	
Bouzelles	27		Bouzelles in billets	
"	28		Marched to Dancehelles arriving in hubs at 11.30 AM. A. Co. arriving in buses from Eyoncourt	
Dancehelles	29		Lieutenant Danielles L.J. perfection	

INTELLIGENCE SUMMARY

(Erase heading not required.)

Instructions regarding War Diaries and Intelligence Summaries are contained in F. S. Regs., Part II. and the Staff Manual respectively. Title Pages will be prepared in manuscript.

Place	Date	Hour	Summary of Events and Information	Remarks and references to Appendices
Dunkirk	July 30		Marched to Landas and entrained for St Omer at 8 PM	
St Omer	31		Detrained here at 4.20 AM and marched to Millam via Watten	

Ernest Montagu
2nd Lt for Adjt 11 H.H.

Aug/16

Army Form C. 2118.

V687

7.v
3 sheets

WAR DIARY
or
INTELLIGENCE SUMMARY.

(Erase heading not required.)

Place	Date	Hour	Summary of Events and Information	Remarks and references to Appendices
MILLAIN	1st Aug		In Billets	
	2nd "		"	
	3rd "	6.45 a.m.	Moved up & at 4.15 a.m. marched to BOLLEZEELE arriving at 6.45 a.m.	
BOLLEZEELE	4th "		In billets - training under Coy. arrangement	
	5th "		"	
	6th "		" Bns.	
	7th "		"	
	8th "		"	
	9th "		"	
	10th "		Inspection by G.O.C. of Kit, Arms, Coy. & Batt. books	
	11th "		In billets training under Bde. arrangements	Bathing at ZEGGARS CAPPEL C.O's parade
	12th "		"	
	13th "		"	
	14th "		"	
	15th "		"	

WAR DIARY
or
INTELLIGENCE SUMMARY.

(Erase heading not required.)

Army Form C. 2118.

Place	Date	Hour	Summary of Events and Information	Remarks and references to Appendices.
BOLLEZEELE	Aug 16th		In billets. Training under Bde. arrangements	
	17th		"	
	18th		"	
	19th		Orders to take over line St Julien from 12th Bde at 5 a.m. Entrained at BOLLEZEELE arriving POPERINGHE at 1:45 p.m. In empty huts until 8:30 p.m. then entrained to YPRES Battn. took over right sub sector.	
	20th		"	
	21st		"	
	22nd		"	
	23rd		Relieved by 10th S.W.B. took over reserve dug-outs on CANAL BANK.	
CANAL BANK	24th		Reserve dug-outs in Canal Bank - working parties furnishing for digging & R.E. work	
	25th		"	
	26th		"	
	27th		"	

Army Form C. 2118.

WAR DIARY
or
INTELLIGENCE SUMMARY.

(Erase heading not required.)

Instructions regarding War Diaries and Intelligence Summaries are contained in F. S. Regs., Part II and the Staff Manual respectively. Title pages will be prepared in manuscript.

Place	Date	Hour	Summary of Events and Information	Remarks and references to Appendices
CANAL BANK	Aug. 28th		Relieved 10th S.W.B. in front line	
	29th		front line	
	30th			
	31st			

Edward Grant
Lt Col (D.S.) 11th S.W.B.
27.9.16

Army Form C. 2118.

WAR DIARY or INTELLIGENCE SUMMARY.
(Erase heading not required.)

Instructions regarding War Diaries and Intelligence Summaries are contained in F. S. Regs., Part II. and the Staff Manual respectively. Title pages will be prepared in manuscript.

Vol 8

11th BATT. SOUTH WALES BORDERERS

Place	Date	Hour	Summary of Events and Information	Remarks and references to Appendices
	Sept.			
FRONT LINE	1.		Relieved by 10th S.W.B. – reserve dug-outs on CANAL BANK.	
CANAL BANK	2.		Reserve dug-outs. Working parties on strong points & Canal Defences.	
"	3.		" " " " " "	
"	4.		" " " " " "	
FRONT LINE	5.		Relieved 10th S.W.B. in front line.	
"	6.		Front line.	
"	7.		Relieved by 13th Welsh 114th Bde. – We relieved 15th Welsh in Left Sector.	
CANAL BANK	8.		Reserve dug-outs on CANAL BANK	
"	9.		Reserve dug-outs LEFT SECTOR.	
"	10.		" " Working parties for through good line	
FRONT LINE	11.		Relieved 10th S.W.B. in front line in daylight.	
"	12.		Front line LEFT SECTOR.	
"	13.		" " " "	
"	14.		Relieved by 10th S.W.B. Artillery bombarded AUN line & cut wire. B Coy relief held up till 12 midnight	

WAR DIARY
or
INTELLIGENCE SUMMARY

Army Form C. 2118.

Place	Date	Hour	Summary of Events and Information	Remarks and references to Appendices
CANAL BANK	Sept. 15th		Reserve dug-outs LEFT SECTOR. Artillery ammunition limbers went at 11 p.m. A Coy wiring party went out to CANADIAN DUG-OUTS. 2nd Lt. G.H.E.G. MOORE wounded.	
"	16th		Reserve dug-outs LEFT SECTOR. Relieved by 16th R.W.F. and took over reserve dug-outs RIGHT SECTOR. 1 Coy 16th held attached to us in lieu of A Coy (unloading rand at Camp E.)	
"	17.		Reserve dug-outs RIGHT SECTOR. Working parties, shortages, burial of fences. 1 Coy 16th held attached. A Coy unloading rand.	
"	18.		As 17th	
"	19.		As 18th	
"	20.		Reserve dug-outs RIGHT SECTOR. Relieved by 10th S.W.B. Conveys by trains to Camp E – arrived 3.15 a.m. 1 Coy 16th held attached. May-packets gone.	
CAMP E.	21.		Working party of 200 out at night. Cable burying.	
"	22.		As 21. Inspected by ARMY COMMANDER (GEN PLUMER) at 3/1 a.m.	
"	23.		MAJOR MORGAN, relieved of C.O.M. at 115th Bde H.Q. at 11 a.m. Working party of 200 Cable burying at night.	

Army Form C. 2118.

WAR DIARY
or
INTELLIGENCE SUMMARY.
(Erase heading not required.)

Instructions regarding War Diaries and Intelligence Summaries are contained in F. S. Regs., Part II. and the Staff Manual respectively. Title pages will be prepared in manuscript.

Place	Date	Hour	Summary of Events and Information	Remarks and references to Appendices
Camp E	Sept. 24		No parades. Cable burying party not out. Changed programme of work with 18th Batt.	
"	25.		Parade 9am - 12 noon - hacking out new trenches - working parties in house-standings in afternoon	
"	26.		as 25th.	
"	27.		as 26th. Col. GAUSSEN in command of Bde.	
"	28.		Parades in afternoon - Cable burying party at night.	
"	29.		as 28th. RND carried out on CANADIAN DUG-OUTS of Grenadiers	
"	30.		Parades in afternoon. Cable burying party at night.	

Lt & Adjutant,
1/1st (Ser.) Bn. S.W. Borderers.

Army Form C. 2118.

Vol 9

WAR DIARY
or
INTELLIGENCE SUMMARY. 11th SWB

(Erase heading not required.)

Instructions regarding War Diaries and Intelligence Summaries are contained in F.S. Regs., Part II and the Staff Manual respectively. Title pages will be prepared in manuscript.

9.V
2 sheet

Place	Date	Hour	Summary of Events and Information	Remarks and references to Appendices
CAMP E	Oct 1.		Training	
	2.		Relieved 13th Welsh on CANAL BANK. Right subsector Right section.	
	3.		17th R.W.F. front line	
FRONT LINE	4.		" front line	
	5.		"	
	6.		"	
	7.		"	
	8.		Relieved by 10th SWB - Support trenches CANAL BANK. C.O. returned from Bde.	
CANAL BANK	9.		Canal Bank - Enemy shelled in neighbourhood of Posts Nos 2.	
	10.		"	
	11.		Relieved 10th SWB in front line	
FRONT LINE	12.		" front line	
	13.		"	
	14.		"	
	15.		Relieved by 13th Welsh moved over to left sector left sub-section in reserve to 10th SWB.	

2353 Wt. W2544/1454 700,000 5/15 D.D.&L. A.D.S.S./Forms/C. 2118.

Army Form C. 2118.

WAR DIARY
or
INTELLIGENCE SUMMARY.
(Erase heading not required.)

Place	Date	Hour	Summary of Events and Information	Remarks and references to Appendices
CANAL BANK	Oct 16		Canal Bank - One dug-out blown in burying 3 men - 2 killed 1 seriously wounded. Working parties supplied for front line.	
	17		Canal Bank. Working parties for front line	
	18		1 Coy sent to support 11th S.W.B. - Working parties	
	19		"	
	20		"	
FRONT LINE	21		Relieved 11th S.W.B. in front line	
	22		Front line	
	23		"	
	24		"	
	25		"	
	26		Relieved by 15th R.W.F. - marched to Camp D. Arrived 3.15 a.m.	
CAMP D	27		Training - Cable burying parties.	
	28		"	
	29		"	
	30		"	
	31		Baths at Camp D.	

(Sgd.) .... a/Adjutant,
11th (Serv:) Bn. S.W. Borderers.

Army Form C. 2118.

WAR DIARY
or
INTELLIGENCE SUMMARY.
(Erase heading not required.)

11th K Batt'n Manchesters

10.V.
7 sheets

Place	Date	Hour	Summary of Events and Information	Remarks and references to Appendices
CAMP. P	Nov. 1.		Training. Working parties on wire-obstacles during day & cable burying in forward area during nights.	
	2.		As for 1st.	
	3.		"	
	4.		Left Camp P for front line. Entrained at PESELHOEK at 4.15 p.m. & proceeded to the Asylum at YPRES. Marched to RED HEART ESTAMINET & drew groundsheets then proceeded to relieve 10th S.W.B. in RIGHT SUBSECTOR of the HILLTOP SECTOR. Relief was complete at 10.20 p.m.	
FRONT LINE	5th-9th		During this time the trenches were very wet: especially the centre portion of the front line where the water was waist deep. The trenches frequently fell in and the repair of these "falls" occupied considerable time daily. Great attention was paid to draining and some new dug-outs were constructed, the ones here and also improved. Patrols went out nightly into the	

WAR DIARY
or
INTELLIGENCE SUMMARY

Army Form C. 2118.

Place	Date	Hour	Summary of Events and Information	Remarks and references to Appendices
hor.			reception of the wounded was	
	5th-9th		awful. - no enemy were encountered. During the above period only 4 cars were sent to the field ambulance as sick now of which and "Trench feet" He suffered no casualties. The enemy was quiet on the whole and their was no marked absence of trouble backers gun fire from 5th-9th. On 9th line was infed by Divisional General.	
	9th		He was relieved by 10th S.W.B. Relief being completed at 9 p.m. The Battn. moved to reserve dug outs in E agar of the open Redoubt.	
Camp Onr.	10th		General "clean up" working parties on Braud Defences during day.	
	11th		General inspection of men and billets by company officers. Working parties on Braud Defences during the day & the Battalion in front line at night.	
	12th		Coy inspections. Work on Braud Defences during the day. Carrying & working parties at night to tranches in the	

Army Form C. 2118.

WAR DIARY
or
INTELLIGENCE SUMMARY
(Erase heading not required.)

Instructions regarding War Diaries and Intelligence Summaries are contained in F.S. Regs., Part II and the Staff Manual respectively. Title pages will be prepared in manuscript.

Place	Date	Hour	Summary of Events and Information	Remarks and references to Appendices
CANAL BANK	12th		front line.	
	13th		Working parties as 12th. Aeroplanes were active during the day. Three hostile planes attacked the Canal but were off by our planes - one was forced down but managed to reach his own lines. Our artillery bombarded (BASHE'S NOSE) (Sheet 28;C;14) heavily at 12.40 a.m.	
	14th		Inspections & cleaning of billets preparatory to handing over to 13th R.W.F. Relieved 15th R.W.F. in support of billets Canal Bank. Left H.Q.M. left billets. Relief complete at 8.40 p.m. Battn. Coy was in billets at TROIS TOUR CHATEAU	
	15th			
FRONT LINE	16th		Relieved 16th R.W.F. in front line. Left seven left billets on relief being complete at 9.45 p.m. From 10 a.m. to 3.30 p.m. the heavy and Divisional Artillery bombarded the enemy's front line and support line	

2353 Wt. W3344/1454 700,000 5/15 L.D.&L. A.D.S.S./Forms/C. 2118.

WAR DIARY
or
INTELLIGENCE SUMMARY

Army Form C. 2118.

Place	Date	Hour	Summary of Events and Information	Remarks and references to Appendices
FRONT LINE	Nov 16th		From C14a.3½.4 to C14a.1.7 (Sheet 28 NW - St Julien), the "Zand Point" arranged previous to a raid on the Stegh Command Redoubt. Shrick damage was done. The enemy's retaliation was both slight and ineffective - about 50 shells in all falling in our area. No material damage was done. 1 man was killed. Our artillery during the day - four enemy "planes" flew over our lines but were driven off by our anti-aircraft fire & no line (N°5 of Hindenb. Rd) were subjected during the bombardment. The same bombardment was carried out on our 16th with the addition that it was repeated from 6 - 6.30 p.m. and from 11 - 11.50 p.m. in conjunction with the artillery supporting the raiding party. From 11.59 - 12.2 midnight 13 trench Mortars fired 70 rounds as a barrage — The enemy's retaliation was greater than on the 16th but very little damage was done.	
	17th			

Army Form C. 2118.

WAR DIARY
or
INTELLIGENCE SUMMARY.
(Erase heading not required.)

Instructions regarding War Diaries and Intelligence Summaries are contained in F.S. Regs., Part II. and the Staff Manual respectively. Title pages will be prepared in manuscript.

Place	Date	Hour	Summary of Events and Information	Remarks and references to Appendices
FRONT LINE	17th		About 150 shells fell in our area.	
	18th		The enemy has been very quiet, only 2 shells fell in our lines. Our artillery carried out a practice SOS signal successfully at 9 p.m.	
	19th		A quiet day. Relieved by 10th S.W.B. relief being complete at 4.30 p.m. Bn moved to billets on Canal Bank. During this time in front line we suffered casualties 3 wounded at billet.	
CANAL BANK	20th 21st 22nd 23rd		Few shell dug-outs were excellent. Bn was in reserve to accomodate to conformers in the battn area. Carrying & wiring parties were supplied to from 1 Bn & Canal Hill/15. two previously entrenched. On the 23rd 150 men were loaded at ELVERDINGHE	
	23rd		We relieved 10th S.W.B. in front line relief being complete at 4 p.m. from 14-23rd inc. 12 cases were evacuated to Field Ambulance as sick, the being a case of "trench foot".	

2353 Wt. W2544/1454 700,000 5/15 D. D. & L. A.D.S.S./Forms/C. 2118.

Army Form C. 2118.

WAR DIARY
or
INTELLIGENCE SUMMARY.
(Erase heading not required.)

11th Batt. S. Lanc. R. (? of [illegible]) Barbara (a heavy [illegible])

Place	Date	Hour	Summary of Events and Information	Remarks and references to Appendices
	Nov.		(a heavy [gunner]) Whilst in rest, one man who was in the front line with the 10th S.L.B. was killed. This was the only casualty in the 11th S.L.B.	
FRONT LINE	26th 27th	2pm	Relieved in the front line by 16th R.W.F. and moved to [Hut?] 5. Arriving in [Camp] about 9pm.	
	27th 28th		General stand-to in Camp.	
	29th		30 minutes intense artillery bombardment of enemy front line opened at 6pm followed by 16th R.W.F. attacking enemy front line (our front area). At 11.50pm received a [?] asking from Brigade when everyone was to turn out from the [?] and fall in ready to move off. The distribution was complete in every detail and ready to move off in 30 minutes. [Enemy] dispersed and carry on as usual.	
	30th		Arrived in the morning as usual. At 2.30pm the Bttn. to ? drawn up on the parade ground in advance to an inspection by the Brig. General Gen. Gen. to Captain Hunter [?]. He [?] hands of the [?] all B'ns	

WAR DIARY
or
INTELLIGENCE SUMMARY.

(Erase heading not required.)

Army Form C. 2118.

11th Batt. South Wales Borderers (2nd Gwent)

Place	Date	Hour	Summary of Events and Information	Remarks and references to Appendices
	30th (cont)		Played the Pilots and played alternately with the Camp C/y Band during the inspection. The G.O.C. Reserves seeing my pleased with everything and addressed the officers and men. The G.O.C. commander presented Artillery medals to men of the Depenses. He was exceedingly nice and most sympathetic in his command Reserves. He then reviewed the Brigade and in referring to the 38th Division Commander expressed his excellent work. Stated that it did him an honour to have in the Brigade scheme and presenting to its rations glory in the coming struggle. The hearts of the men were too soft for the 38th but were just and to emphasize this conclusion of each battalion during a few rifle movements.	

M Edwards Capt
& Adjutant,
11th (Ser.) Bn. S.W. Borderers.

Army Form C. 2118.

WAR DIARY
or
INTELLIGENCE SUMMARY
(Erase heading not required.)

Vol XI

1/4 Lancs Fusiliers Officer Commanding (or Major) (or Lieut.) December 1916.

Place	Date	Hour	Summary of Events and Information	Remarks and references to Appendices
Dranoutre Reserve	1916 Dec 1		The Battalion was still in camp in Dranoutre Reserve. The GOC 86th Inf Bde visited the camp and expressed himself as very pleased with the excellent sanitary arrangements of the camp and its cleanliness. He expressed the opinion that the field kitchens were much more handy than the dixies, inasmuch as kept on hand twenty-two Cooks carrying parties were much to Butler.	
	2			
	3		Divine Service in the morning.	
			The Commanding Officer Lieut Col McGowan CMG DSO proceeded on leave until 8.1.17. Major J H Morgan assumed command of the Battalion and Capt J M Mortlock assumed 2nd in command.	
Support Right Sub Sector	4		The Battalion carried on with training in the camp.	
	5		The Battalion left Camp E and marched to Camp F and entrance for YPRES. & debussed at Ypres	
	6		Asylum and marched to the Canal Bank to relieve the 1st Herts Battalion in support of Right subsector right section. Relief was complete about 8pm. Most of the Battalion employed furnishing working parties to repair on Canal Bank spare time remaining its entire employed carrying ammn to front line in preparation for	

Army Form C. 2118.

WAR DIARY
or
INTELLIGENCE SUMMARY

(Erase heading not required.)

11th Service Bn. Sherwood Foresters (Notts & Derby) December 1916

Instructions regarding War Diaries and Intelligence Summaries are contained in F. S. Regs., Part II. and the Staff Manual respectively. Title Pages will be prepared in manuscript.

Place	Date 1916 Dec	Hour	Summary of Events and Information	Remarks and references to Appendices
	7		Kept parties in charge of 100 men all excellent work, over 400 yards of new made into front line. Battalion responses to construct side.	
	8		The morning of previous night was carried on by the 10th S.W.B. Battalion headquarters at IRISH FARM, to relieve the 10th S.W.B.	
	9		Our companies in front line cut off from each other by any owing to trenches being waterlogged. 2nd Lancashire and 2nd West Kent two at TUSPIN to protect and reconnoitre cages in front. The night was very light making approach difficult. Nothing special was reported. The same night 2nd Lt. Whyte with 10 O.R. patrolled NO MAN'S LAND with a view to finding and fighting any teams who might be there. No name of teams Kept to their own side of the parapet.	
	10		The Enemy shelled MELTJE held by the 13th Division heavily during the day, also Britain's support no mans land without meeting any of the enemy.	
	11		Nothing happened during the day with the Hunters.	
	12		We were relieved by the 12th Sussex battalion 39th Division which were taken over to line from the 39th Division. The battalion marched to Camp E and stayed there for one night only.	
Elverdinghe Defences.	13		Left Camp E and marched to take over the Elverdinghe defences. The battalion the two companies were billeted at Machine Gun Farm / and as Belgian Chateau	
	14		Elverdinghe Defences, working parties applied to work in defences.	
	15		Elverdinghe Defences, the men were comfortable and had quite a restful time.	

Army Form C. 2118.

WAR DIARY
or
INTELLIGENCE SUMMARY
(Erase heading not required.)

1/1K Bn H Wales [Regiment] (2nd Garrison) December 1916

Place	Date 1916 Dec	Hour	Summary of Events and Information	Remarks and references to Appendices
Elverdinghe Defences	16		Voluntary Divine Service at M.G. Farm.	
	17		At dusk the battalion was relieved in the Elverdinghe defences by the Cardiff City battalion. The battalion then moved to ROUSSEL FARM which is situated about a mile from Elverdinghe on the Elverdinghe–Eperlecques road. Here the men were billeted in huts, huts of unlikely taken over from the French. The camp was officially closed and its inmates deemed to have no long had running parallel to the road which was three companies.	
Roussel Farm	18		The dud shew of musketry etc differing somewhat from that of the First Army and consequent intervention of pulper parties employed in making alterations etc. Major T. Keegan left the battalion temporarily to command a Musketry section 2nd Army School at TILQUES. Capt A.H. Montes [Monks] is assumed command. Sgt W. Williams assumed 2nd in command of battalion. Photographers applied to work with the front and support lines of BOESINGHE sector.	
	19			
	20		10 Apl 1916. Preparing for move on 22nd.	
	21			
	22		At 6 am the battalion left Roussel Farm Camp and marched to Eperlecques station where it entrained for STOMER, also the following attachments to pioneer courses. HQ OR TILQUES School. 60 OR TERDEGHEM Bombing school. 24 OR MONTRECATS Sniping. 15 OR BERTHWEN. The battalion marched from STOMER to TATINGHEM. Here the men were completely billeted in barns etc where they were able to have good stows telling on the progress of being out of the trenches. Everyone felt particularly pleased at the prospect of being out of the trenches over Xmas.	

WAR DIARY or INTELLIGENCE SUMMARY

Army Form C. 2118.

11th South Wales Borderers (2nd Gwent) December 1916

Place	Date	Hour	Summary of Events and Information	Remarks and references to Appendices
Méteren	23		Reporting day man spent in general cleaning up and inspection parades.	
	24		Company religious services. The C of E service was held in a good sized building. He had band in attendance playing appropriate Xmas hymns. Draft of 99 recruits arrived.	
	25		Being Xmas Day there the men were rather idle to pass the hours as nothing like the custom of this reserve and every effort was made to make its Xmas dinner an event of the day. Turkey and plum pudding by the dinner and there were sufficient of these and lots of pork not potatoes and green vegetables. Every man at 100 [?] received divers. At the evening all the officers of the battalion dined together.	
			It was very breezy and good people everyone content and thankful not to be in the trenches.	
	26		The Battalion went to baths at STOMER. In the afternoon 50 men were sent on a fatigue party to the 2nd Army School WISQUES.	
	27		60 men supplied as a fatigue party to 2nd Army School. The remainder of battalion employed in tidying up billets etc. Casualty Keith Coats Brown arrived on arrival of battalion was Capt AM Monteith who arrived 23rd on command.	
	28		60 men under Capt 2/Lt Helmsman and 2/Lt Sheers employed to assist to dismantle close the encampment was placed with the greatest remnants. Training under battalion arrangements.	
	29		Battalion training as per scheme. Regimental canteen opened as to sale of tea, cake, cigarettes etc.	

Army Form C. 2118.

WAR DIARY
or
INTELLIGENCE SUMMARY

(Erase heading not required.)

11th South Wales Borderers (2nd Gwent) December 1916

Place	Date	Hour	Summary of Events and Information	Remarks and references to Appendices
Jerusalem	1916 Dec 30		Parades for training as usual. The last day of the training was spent in football matches in which every man played. The trophy match was quite a dashing affair. Everyone enjoys the games immensely.	
	31		Divine Service for C of E held as usual. Inspection none see for R.C. on the ridge church.	

W. Edwards
Capt. & Adjt.
for O.C. 11th S.W. Borderers

Army Form C. 2118.

WAR DIARY
or
INTELLIGENCE SUMMARY.
(Erase heading not required.)

11th S.W.B.

January 1916.

Place	Date	Hour	Summary of Events and Information	Remarks and references to Appendices
Tidworth			Battalion still at Tidworth. In the evening a concert was held for the men in the Recreation Room. He had played selections and gave good items and are supplied by the men — the instruments being contributed chiefly by one of the men newly arrived from England.	
	2.1.16		H. Battery sermons on route, heavy — going to church to obtain rest with a chaplain. In the afternoon of the 5th so many men so fewest miles to St. Swan to its intention on Lower Swan, spreading mischief in the Army.	
	6th		Ordinary routine of the 6th morning of the 6th Battalion orders for this day contained the following announcements The Commanding Officer has the great pleasure in announcing the promotion —	
			Lower Eagle January 2nd 1916. Capt. Swan Swan, R.A.M.C. dated 11th Jul/18 11/216 Sgt. Evans S. A Cy 11th Jul/18 Capt. C. Tommy S Cy 11th Aug/8	Military Cross Distinguished Mentioned in Despatches
	7th		The Commanding Officer received from a source at the GOC 59 Welsh Division	

12.V.
6 sheets

WAR DIARY / INTELLIGENCE SUMMARY

Army Form C. 2118

Place: [Etaples?]
Month: January 1917

Date	Hour	Summary of Events and Information	Remarks
7th		Assumed command of the Battalion. Rode to Calshores [?]	
8th		Enemy Hd Qrs. In the afternoon the officers & as many men as possible marched to St Omer to witness a performance of "The Bodies on the Road." This proved to be a most clever & amusing performance arranged and acted by the men of the D.B. ASC Motor Transport. Heavy rain fell during the march back & billets	
9-10-11-12th		Battalion exercises in with the training according to scheme.	
12th		Draft of 19 men joined the Battalion	
13th		Training. New draft proceeded to 29th Divn. Reinforcement Camp to perfect training	
14th		Sunday. Divine Service	
15.16.17.18.		Training	
19th		Very cold & frosty	
20th		Beginning to be more not very bad for time. Battalion left Etaples and marched to St Omer where it entrained to Strazeele from Strazeele the Battalion marched to "D" Camp near Locker.	
21st		Battalion stores left Etaples at 12 noon being transported by lorries	

WAR DIARY or INTELLIGENCE SUMMARY

Army Form C. 2118.

January 1917

Place	Date	Hour	Summary of Events and Information	Remarks and references to Appendices
G Camp	21st		The country side was white with snow & made skating good.	
	22nd		Battalion transport arrived at Steenwyck having taken two days to complete the journey. The first night transport reached Steenwoorde where it stayed for the night.	
Poval Farm	23		Batt'n marched to Poval Farm.	
	24		Two OR's & Officers moving to relieve the 1/8th Loyal North Lancs. Officers being conducted from Elverdinghe to Koesten. On return of this party at 1pm Batt'n HQ and transport went to Brewery sect'n relieving the Buoy Cy Battalion at Black Farm, which battalion moved into front line.	
Black Farm	25		No companies in as L line. 15 companies at Black Farm and C company at Canal East. Working parties found for work under RE etc carrying material to front line. Track still very wet, roads slimey & slippery.	
	26		B the enemy one company moved to Parity & Officers took up ats forward positions then returned to billets. One Company moved to extreme night of Railway embankment between X King and Lone Pile Camel.	

WAR DIARY
or
INTELLIGENCE SUMMARY

Army Form C. 2118.

January 1917

Place	Date	Hour	Summary of Events and Information	Remarks and references to Appendices
Hulluch Sector	27th		The weather still cold & freezing hard. Working parties to front line.	
	28		Cold, clear day. Major Keats Brown assumed command 12th Royal Sussex Regt. Major J.M. Hensealth assumed 2nd in command, 7th Batt. Battalion.	
Baraque Chatier			(the incoming Battalion moved into front line and relieved the (Saint Cly Battalion) two companies held to front line and to rest of line and one Co. in the Baraque Chatier. This was the first time the Battalion relieved the Royal Sussex. Our front line was on top of the Canal Bank, and facing the German front line was on a similar position on the other side, the distance between the lines being about 50 yards. The cold weather still frozen the Canal hard. Weather still bitterly cold. Enemy fired Baraque Chatier enclosure roughly.	
	29		but no damage was done.	
	30		About 1 30am Enemy commenced a fierce bombardment into Belgian Battery on our left. When transport lights enemy machine gun fire attempted to enter Belgian trenches but were repulsed. Enemy batteries opened onto Prosper.	

WAR DIARY
or
INTELLIGENCE SUMMARY.

January 1917

Place	Date	Hour	Summary of Events and Information	Remarks and references to Appendices
Boesinghe Chateau	30th		Enemy threw bombs trying to get on the canal on our left and a man to his hop the rise. We are known over the trees and my men made holes were made.	
			Liason established with Belgians on our left — About 9pm a Gen. Headen being wounded. The 1st Regt of Infantry (Belgians) were divery to relieve us on my left.	
	31st		Enemy shelled the village & surroundings fairly slightly. No damage was done. Lt. Col. Duncan (My. Gen. Hickie)(LB.S.D o ADC ↔) makes the funk line in the morning.	

1.2.17

(signed) Whimms
(signed left to OC 11th Battalion)

Army Form C. 2118.

February 1917

Vol / 3

WAR DIARY
or
INTELLIGENCE SUMMARY
(Erase heading not required.)

11th South Wales Borderers (2nd Gwents)

Instructions regarding War Diaries and Intelligence Summaries are contained in F. S. Regs., Part II. and the Staff Manual respectively. Title Pages will be prepared in manuscript.

13.V.
7 shut

Place	Date	Hour	Summary of Events and Information	Remarks and references to Appendices
Bescinghe	1st		Battalion was in the front line of the Bescinghe Sector. The day was dull in the morning, brightening up in the afternoon rendering visibility good. From 8am till dusk our artillery carried out a programme of bombardment of enemy lines. Opposite our sector all guns on the distant ridge were the 9.2 guns and over 1000 shells, the 5 in guns 2000, the field artillery medium trench mortars & stokes many a very large amount of ammunition. The shooting was excellent and enemy defences, trench lines & parapets, wire etc. were very badly damaged.	
	2nd		Until 4 o'clock enemy was comparatively quiet, then he commenced an organised retaliation of minenwerfer, L.H.V. N.2. and 5.9 guns which was concentrated on the S. line. Wings & & Bescinghe Chateau wood. Bombardment being in much evasion and tapered and lasted about 2 hours. The rest of morning at 11 am this was repeated similarly for 1½ an hour and again at 6am and then at intervals throughout the day. Casualties were 4 killed + 12 wounded.	
			At dusk Battalion was relieved by 17th R.W.F. after which Battalion moved to Forest Farm crossing the canal open.	
Forest Farm	3rd		300 men left camp about 7.30 am to work on new Railway from Elverdinghe to Woesten.	
"	4th		Sunday - Divine Service	
"	5th		About 120 men had baths at Elverdinghe & their clothes disinfected Weather cold & clear. Working parties for Railway Construction. Apps.	

Army Form C. 2118.

WAR DIARY
or
INTELLIGENCE SUMMARY

(Erase heading not required.)

1st South Wales Borderers (2nd Garrison)   February 1917

Instructions regarding War Diaries and Intelligence Summaries are contained in F. S. Regs, Part II. and the Staff Manual respectively. Title Pages will be prepared in manuscript.

Place	Date	Hour	Summary of Events and Information	Remarks and references to Appendices
Burcat Sam	6		Very cold morning. The Corps Commander Lieut-General the Hon. Sir Julian Byng paid a surprise visit to the camp about 11 am and held an informal inspection. Cleared to find no every man ready to move off - very few men were in camp at the time. The Corps Commander then visited the men in gas drill hut, he inspected most of the men just in their blouses with gas respirators and accepted the drill was done very smartly. He then inspected each man's ammunition - also three Lewis gun ammunition - he appeared to be very pleased with the cleanliness.	
Blewit Farm	7		The afternoon battalion moved into Blewit Farm to relieve the 16th Welsh (Cardiff City Battalion) in support. Relief complete at 5 pm. The Major General (Division Commander) accompanied by the Brigadier General visited the support area.	
	8		In the afternoon Major Delaby (2nd Welsh) arrived to take over command of the Battalion. He left however that evening, unable to ditto. Move carried on party in the X line and party in front line numbers the operation of the REs.	
	9th		Companies carried out as much training as possible - Bayonet Exercise Bombs, Signals drill etc. Evening - Musketry, Bayonet fighting - Section in undertaken Working parties to front line.	

WAR DIARY or INTELLIGENCE SUMMARY

Army Form C. 2118.

February 1917

11th South Wales Borderers (2nd Gwent)

Place	Date	Hour	Summary of Events and Information	Remarks and references to Appendices
Blaret Dam	10		Moved into front line and relieved 10th Welsh (Rhondda City) Battalion. Relief complete 8pm – very quiet night – thaw commenced	
Front line	11		Quiet day	
"	12		Day quiet, at night enemy bombing the ice on the canal and appeared to be very nervous	
"	13		During the day, enemy bombarded heavily south trench mortars, 4.H.V. 4.2 and 5.9 guns, village of Boesinghe Station & road, and Battalion HQrs. During this bombardment our men were killed in the village or the Battalion HQrs. Enemy's snipers and the battalion was fortunate not to have had many more casualties.	
"	14		During the day some added considerable wire entanglement. 5 enemy planes attacked 2 of ours and secured in bringing one down behind our lines. The officer pilot was killed	
			Rifles at the front line the 17th R.W.F. and battalion moved to Forest Camp, nearby 1 Major General Plunketts made the camp and inspected huts, latrines etc.	
Forest Camp	15		300 men went to assist in Railway Construction work.	
			Late afternoon a very exciting aerial fight was seen from Forest Camp. A German plant which circled our lines over attacked by one of ours.	
			Our plane flew directly for the enemy plane, they first dived underneath at at the same time Lewis Gun the German officer was killed	

WAR DIARY
or
INTELLIGENCE SUMMARY

Army Form C. 2118.

February 1917

Place	Date	Hour	Summary of Events and Information	Remarks and references to Appendices
	15		and the planes dived to earth in flames. It fell in a field between the camp and Elverdinghe. The pilot was moving the Iron Cross. At 7.30pm enemy suddenly shelled Forest Farm with 5.9" guns. There being absolutely no protection in the camp, the men were immediately ordered to transfer to the planks but unfortunately one company was caught by a salvo which inflicted many casualties. (4 men killed, 18 wounded, 5 of whom have since died).	
Forest Farm	16-17		Two companies remained in these trenches for the night and 2 companies + Hqrs moved to. and others Forton Farm area with the 151 Co. RE. This migration was necessary until battalion moved into bigger at Billet Farm on Sunday. During the time at Forton Farm saw and trained men considered in no man's land.	
Billet Farm	18		Relief 10th South (at Billet Farm) in Support.	
	19		Lieut Colonel Parris (10th Yorkshire Regt) arrived to take command of the Battalion. Major (Temp Lieut Colonel) McGowan CMG DSO	
	20		Companies moving in company areas. Lieut - Colonel McGowan CMG DSO left to rejoin the Second Army	Battalion
	21		Very dull and misty throughout the day - enabled the ration work to be rendered and the enemy were very quiet, the usual working parties for ... under RE ... by the Battalion.	

Army Form C. 2118.

WAR DIARY
INTELLIGENCE SUMMARY
(Erase heading not required.)

11th [North?] [illegible] Battalion (2nd [illegible])

February 1917

Place	Date	Hour	Summary of Events and Information	Remarks and references to Appendices
Flewt [illegible]	22		Slight rain, very quiet day. In the evening 2 patrols moved into front line to relieve 1st Btlgns.	
Front line	23		Relief complete 5.30pm. Quiet night. Spent time very misty and visibility practically nil. Advantage of this mildly conditions was taken for moving "S" line erecting camouflage &c. Enemy was enterprising, opposite to Belgian Regiment on our left, took in front line and Belgium Regiment Postes Bleu being made [illegible] Colonel [illegible] Radio. The sector on our left was held by the 1st Company 1st Regiment of Carbineers.	
	24		Quiet day.	
	25		Only enemy activity, occurrence of harassing sniping at 9pm on Knuckle and Ridge of [illegible] Shelled, doing no damage. [illegible] The 9th Carabiniers was relieved by the 2nd Carabiniers.	
	26		At 4pm enemy commenced T.Mortar bombard west of 5 line village and [illegible] Chateau grounds, a few shrapnel were sent over [illegible] Village at about the same time. Firing died down until 5.25pm. The retaliation with 240's Newton & Aeron Trench Mortars Rifle Grenades was felt in our lines. 10 pound Shells & 4.5 howitzers, evening kept up west at rest & there was no much [illegible] In the evening Battalion was relieved by 17th RWF and moved to X Camp.	

Army Form C. 2118.

WAR DIARY
or
INTELLIGENCE SUMMARY
(Erase heading not required.)

11th (Sovt) Militia (Yorks) (2nd Event)

February 1917

Place	Date	Hour	Summary of Events and Information	Remarks and references to Appendices
X Camp	27		A model camp, quite the best the battalion has occupied in the Poperinghe area. The huts are comparatively situated, warm enough and comfortable. 300 men supplied as working party in Railway construction.	
-	28		Working party of 300 men in Railway Construction. 1 Company however went Coy. Training. 8 NCO's interested in bombing. 48 men Lewis Gun.	

M. Murdoch Capt & Adjutant,
for O.C. 11th (Serv) Bn. S.W. Borderers.

WAR DIARY
INTELLIGENCE SUMMARY
(Erase heading not required.)

Army Form C. 2118.

11th South Wales Borderers (3rd Lovat) February 1917

Place	Date	Hour	Summary of Events and Information	Remarks and references to Appendices
Medical Resumé for month ending 28.2.17				

The health of the Battalion has been very good and compares not unfavourably with other Battalions of the Division.

A fair amount of care has to be given to render the hut sanitary, latrine buckets and urine tubs placed at frequent intervals along the whole front line.

Considerable difficulty was experienced in supplying the Battalion with water. A ruinous Village being some company grounds to procure water, this water has to be chlorinated.

A mild epidemic of catarrhal influenza appeared in this winter. There was a large diminution of P.U.O. cases as compared to finds in other sectors held by the division.

It is a fact worthy of note that this winter was less exposed with cases than the Hill Top and Lancashire farm sectors.

.... & Adjutant,
11th (Serv.) Bn. S.W. Borderers.

to O.C

Army Form C. 2118.

WAR DIARY
or
INTELLIGENCE SUMMARY

(Erase heading not required.)

11th Ser: Bn South Wales Borderers (2nd Gwent)   Vol 14

14.V.
3 sheet

Place	Date	Hour	Summary of Events and Information	Remarks and references to Appendices
X Camp	1917 March 1st		Concert in Church Army Hut. Batt; band present.	
"	" 2nd		Working parties on Railway Construction. Working parties on Railway Construction. Afterwards marched direct to Elverdinghe defences, and L. Line. H.Q. moved to Machine Gun Farm.	
Machine Gun Farm	" 3rd		Disposition of Batt: 2 Coys. less 1 platoon in Elverdinghe; 2 platoons at L.2; 2 platoons at L.3; 2 platoons at L.4; 2 platoons at L.8; 1 platoon at L.10.	
"	" 4th		Divine Services held at M.G. Farm — R.C.; C.E.; and Nonconformist. Every man put through Lachrymatory Gas test.	
"	" 5th		Heavy fall of snow. Work on defences. Training carried on with Lewis Gun, Bombing, Rapid loading, and Box Respirators.	
"	" 6th		Training programme carried on with Lewis Gun, Bombing, Rifle Grenades, Box Respirators.	
"	" 7-10		Training in use of various weapons — Lewis Gun, Bombs, Rifle Grenades, Bayonet Fighting, Rapid Arming and loading.	
"	" 11th		Commanding Officer left for course at 2nd Army School. Major Monteith assumed command of the Batt:	
"	" 12th		Dull day. Working parties on L.3. Training of Specialists.	

Army Form C. 2118.

WAR DIARY
or
INTELLIGENCE SUMMARY

(Erase heading not required.)

11th Ser: Bn South Wales Borderers (2nd Gwent)

Instructions regarding War Diaries and Intelligence Summaries are contained in F.S. Regs., Part II. and the Staff Manual respectively. Title Pages will be prepared in manuscript.

Place	Date	Hour	Summary of Events and Information	Remarks and references to Appendices
Machine Gun Farm	Feb 1917 14-16		Batt'n H.Q. at Machine Gun Farm. Training of specialists carried on. Working parties on L defences.	
"	17th		Commanding Officer (Lt Col Radice) returned from course at 2nd Army School.	
"	18th		Divine services held at Machine Gun Farm. Batt'n relieved by 17th R.W.F. Batt'n relieved 16th Welsh in support line — relief completed at 10 pm. Wiring of "S" line.	
Bleuet Farm	19th		Batt'n H.Q. at Bleuet Farm. Working parties under R.E. and wiring of "S" and "X" lines.	
"	20th		30 shells (shrapnel) fell round Bleuet Farm, and values were fired on to a battery in rear of Bleuet. One man wounded.	
"	21st		Heavy fall of snow during night. Working parties provided.	
"	22nd		Relieved 16th Welsh in front line. Relief completed at 9.30 pm. Wiring and working parties. Very quiet night.	
FRONT LINE	23rd		Very quiet. During the afternoon the following places were heavily shelled with trench mortars — Village St, Church, between Hunter and Bridge St.	

Army Form C. 2118.

WAR DIARY
— or —
INTELLIGENCE SUMMARY

(Erase heading not required.)

11th Ser. Bn. South Wales Borderers (2nd Gwent)

Instructions regarding War Diaries and Intelligence Summaries are contained in F. S. Regs., Part II. and the Staff Manual respectively. Title Pages will be prepared in manuscript.

Place	Date	Hour	Summary of Events and Information	Remarks and references to Appendices
FRONT LINE	May 1917 24th		Quiet night day.	
"	25th		At 3 am Heavy bombardment on our left (Belgian Area). Bulgarians raided enemy trenches, killed a large number of Germans, and brought back 6 prisoners. Wiring parties out. S. line. Quiet night.	
"	26th		Relieved by 16th Welsh. Relief completed 10.30 pm.	
BLEVET FARM	27th		Batt HQ at Blevet Farm. Working and wiring parties.	
"	28th		At Blevet Farm.	
"	29th		At 3.30 am heavy bombardment on our right and left. Provided R.E. working and wiring parties.	
"	30th		Relieved 16th Welsh in front line. Relief completed at 10 pm. At midnight raid carried out on our right — 1 prisoner captured.	
FRONT LINE	31st		Enemy heavily shelled our front line between 9.30 am — 10 am. Much damage done to front line — two slight casualties. Our retaliation effective.	

J Mountolief Pryor
for Lt. Col. [illegible]

WAR DIARY or INTELLIGENCE SUMMARY

Army Form C. 2118.

(Erase heading not required)

1st Battalion Irish Rifles (attached 16th Division)

Vol 75

Place	Date	Hour	Summary of Events and Information	Remarks and references to Appendices
BOESINGHE Sector	1917 April 30		G.O.C. VIII CORPS toured front line at 12 noon. The enemy shelled Fr. Liebst work heavy and between French Mortars between 4.45 P.M. and 6 p.m. Our heavies and Regt. Trench Mortars retaliated on same as the Field Artillery on Enemy Artillery. Nos 1 and 2 Posts were destroyed and some enemy in our Communication Trench. The 16th Welch Regiment relieved the Battalion in the front trenches by 10.10 p.m. Left between "A" By & Twin Dykes. Support disposition:- HQ at Essex Farm; "A" Coy & "Twin Dykes"; "D" Coy – "X" and Left, "C" Coy - Roger Farm, "B" Coy - Marie Farm, Left. G.O.C. 39th Division visited line.	
BLEUET FARM	" 4 " 6th		Major E.J. de P. O'KELLY, Royal Welsh Fusiliers joined & took command Major MONTEITH took over command of "B" Coy.	
"	" 7th		The Battalion relieved the 16th Welsh Regiment in the front line by 10.7 p.m. The 16 Welsh Regiment moving into Support - Dispositions - Battalion HQ at BOESINGHE CHATEAU. "B" Company Front Line right, "C" Company Front Line left; "A" Company MAPP E St; "D" Company BOESINGHE WOOD.	

Army Form C. 2118.

WAR DIARY
or
INTELLIGENCE SUMMARY.

(Erase heading not required.)

Instructions regarding War Diaries and Intelligence Summaries are contained in F. S. Regs., Part II. and the Staff Manual respectively. Title pages will be prepared in manuscript.

_____ 11th Battalion _____ A/H Welsh Borderers (2nd Gwent)

Place	Date	Hour	Summary of Events and Information	Remarks and references to Appendices
BESSINGHE SECTOR	May 8th		Battalion "Tea" Gas Alarm at 3 p.m.	
	10th		Heavy shooting at 9 p.m. Commenced laying wires out from Battalion H.Q. — Signal Office, St Mihiel P.	
	13th		G.O.C. VIII Corps visited H.Q. Posn. at 5 p.m. The Battalion was relieved by 16th Welsh Regt. by 10 p.m. and moved into Support dispositions, A.P. — RUBET FARM; "B" Company "X" (Left Right) and "C" Company "X" line left. H.B. — MARIE JEANNE. Coy "D" Coy at ROGER FARM.	
RUBET FARM	14th		Divisional Car for return at 3 p.m. Coys were unable to get the showers at _____. Can not be heard.	
	15th		B.G.C. 115th Brigade presented Northern & the following — Capt. Evan Evans RAMC Military Cross 2nd.97 Major WYATT J.G. 38620 Bronze M.M.S.E.A. 91633 716 Lewis. H. Military Medal	
	17th		Lt. Col. A. H. RM.) C.E. proceeded to Hill Copse School Major Edge P. O'Kelly assumed temporary command of the Battalion	
	19th		The Battalion was relieved by 17th Royal Welsh Fusiliers and moved to A.P. "L" in new dispositions. H.Q. — MACHINE GUN FARM (LB), H. Company L.A., 1 Platoon

WAR DIARY
or
INTELLIGENCE SUMMARY

Army Form C. 2118.

11th Battn 2nd Mon Brigade 3rd Div [?]

Place	Date	Hour	Summary of Events and Information	Remarks and references to Appendices
	Apr			
MACHINE GUN COYS	27th		and 1 L.G. — L8, D Coy, 2 Platoons. 1 Platoon and 1 L.G. — L3. 1 Platoon and L.3. B + C Companies One Platoon as REIGERSBERG, EVERDINGHE. Major MONTEITH — Adjutant Commdg Standing Patrol. Major Lieut G. NORTON, Royal Scots Fusiliers joined as Acting Adjut. Lieut — Col. Mr. ROYDS assumed command of Battalion.	
"	28th		HQ and A and D Coys were relieved by parties of the 55th Division and moved into the EVERDINGHE defences as Brigade Reserve. HQ Elverdinghe Château formed A and D Coys — BUSEL FARM.	

G.S. Cadwell Lieut Colonel,
Commanding 11th Bn [?] Fusiliers

Copy..2......

Battalion Orders No 15.
by
Lieut Colonel A.H. Radice.
Commanding 11th Service Battalion South Wales Borderers.(2nd Gwent.)
13-4-17.

---

1. The Battalion will be relieved in the front line this evening by the 16th Welsh Regt.

2. On being relieved Companies will move independently to the BLEUET FARM area.

3. The disposition of the Battalion in the BLEUET FARM area will be as under :-

Battalion Hqrs.	Bleuet Farm.
B. Company.	X. Line (Right).
C. Company.	X. Line (Left).
A. Company.	BARN ~~Emile~~ Farm Area.
D. Company.	Paradou Farm.

4. One Officer and one N.C.O. per Company will proceed to take over at 5 pm today.
   O's C. Companies will arrange that blankets and kits are drawn from Battalion Storeroom at BLEUET FARM and taken to Company areas.
   No kits or blankets to be carried from BLEUET FARM before 8-15 pm.

5. Trench maps, trench code books, instructions regarding work and all information regarding front line will be handed over and receipts passed. Lewis Gun Magazines will not be handed over.

6. Traffic regulations will be strictly complied with.- ALL PARTIES going out of the line to proceed via HUNTER STREET. BRIDGE STREET must be kept clear for incoming Unit.

7. Relief complete to be reported to Battalion Hqrs by RUNNER.

8. Working parties will be supplied as per table to be issued later.

9. O.C. A. Company will render a certificate to Orderly Room by 9 am 14th inst., that all ranks know the positions to be occupied in the X. Line South of the Railway if required.

10. Receipts re cleanliness etc., must be passed and sent to Orderly Room by 9 am. 14th inst.,

[signature]
Capt & Adjt.
11th South Wales Borderers.

Copy No 1. File.
      2. 115th Infy Bde.
      3. 16th Welsh.
      4. A. Company.
      5. B.   "
      6. C.   "
      7. D.   "
      8. T.O. and A/Q.M.

THESE OPERATION ORDERS ARE TO BE DESTROYED IMMEDIATELY AFTER RELIEF.

Copy No. 2

Battalion Orders No 16.
by
Major E.J.De.P.O'Kelly.
Commanding 11th Service Battalion South Wales Borderers.(2nd Gwent)
18-4-17.

---

1. The Battalion will be relieved in the Support Area on night of 19th/20th inst., and will relieve the 17th Royal Welsh Fusiliers in the L.Line.
2. Dispositions of the Battalion in the L.Line will be as follows :-
   A. Coy. 11th S.W.B. will relieve D. Coy 17th R.W.F.
       at L.4. Company Hqrs and 2 platoons.
       at L.8. (Burgomaster Farm). 1 Platoon and 1 L.G.Sect.
   B. Coy. 11th S.W.B. will relieve A. Company 17th R.W.F.
       at Chateau Grounds,ELVERDINGHE. Coy Hqrs and 2 platoons.
       at B. and C. Blockhouses. "   . 1 Platoon and L.G.Sect.
   C. Coy. 11th S.W.B. will relieve D. Coy 17th R.W.F.
       at Chateau Grounds ELVERDINGHE. 1 Platoon and L.G.Sect.
       at Block A. House B.   "   . 1 Platoon.
       at REIGERSBURG CHATEAU.   1. Platoon.
   D. Coy. 11th S.W.B. will relieve C. Company 17th R.W.F.
       at L.2. Company Hqrs and 2 platoons.
       at Machine Gun Farm. 1 Platoon and L.G.Section.
   Battalion Headquarters. Machine Gun Farm.
3. An Advance Party of 1 Officer and 24 O.Rs.will proceed to take over Company Hqrs and Company Posts at 5 pm.
4. B. and C. Companies will be relieved in the X. Line at about 6 pm. On relief they will proceed to ELVERDINGHE via HUNTER STREET.
   A. and D. Companies will be relieved in the BLEUET FARM area commencing 8-45 pm.
   Traffic regulations will be strictly complied with.
5. Receipts for cleanliness of Billets and Company areas will be passed and rendered to Orderly Room by 10 am. 20th inst.,
6. In the event of an AAlarm during relief, Companies will take up the nearest defensive positions and report to the nearest Company or Battalion Hqrs.
7. Trench maps, Instructions regarding work and all other information will be handed and taken over and receipts passed.
8. All Companies will man their posts on taking over and ensure that all ranks know their positions in case of attack. A report that this has been done will be rendered to Orderly Room by 10 am., 20th inst.,
9. Completion of relief will be reported to Battalion Hqrs in Code.

Capt & Adjt.

11th South Wales Borderers.(2nd Gwent.)

THESE OPERATION ORDERS ARE TO BE DESTROYED ON COMPLETION OF RELIEF.

Copy No 1. File.
2. 115th Infy Bde.
3. 17th R.W.F.
4. A. Coy.
5. B. Coy.
6. C. Coy.
7. D. Coy.
8. T.O. and A/Q.M.

XXXVIII

Vol 16

Army Form C. 2118.

WAR DIARY
or
INTELLIGENCE SUMMARY.

11th Service Battalion (not Required) Royal Irish Fusiliers (2nd Gwent)

Place	Date	Hour	Summary of Events and Information	Remarks and references to Appendices
ELVERDINGHE	1917 May 1st	4 PM	Battalion moved to BOLLEZEELE area for training. Entrained at BRANDHOEK (Sheet 28 G 12 c 6.9). Detrained ESQUELBEC. Marched to BOLLEZEELE and billeted in southern portion of village. Transport marched from their lines to BOLLEZEELE. Lieut Col. R. H. Raikes granted leave to 15/5/17. Major E.J. de P. O'KELLY assumed temporary command of the Battalion	
BOLLEZEELE	" 6th			
"	" 7th		Lt-Gen HUNTER-WESTON commanding VIII Corps saw the Battalion march past in front	
"	" 11th		Maj-Gen Blacklock, commanding 38th Div inspected the Battalion while training.	
"	" 12th		Lt-Gen Plumer Commanding 2nd Army inspected the Battalion while training.	
"	" 16th	7.30am	Marched to HOUTKERQUE and billeted there. Lt Col R.H Raikes resumed command of the Battalion.	
HOUTKERQUE	May 3? 18th		Battalion marched from HOUTKERQUE to M Camp SHEET 27. F.27.c.	
M Camp	" 19th		Moved into Support BOESINGHE Sector relieving the 14th Welsh Regiment. Bn HQ Blunt Farm; A Coy X line (my Lo); D Coy X line (Sept); C Coy at ROGER FARM; B Coy at MARIE JEANNE Cot. Relief completed at 12.15 pm	
SHEET FARM 27th			No 22177 Sgt Hammersley D Coy, and No 21750 4/Cpl Parish, Lewis Gunner Coy, were mentioned in GEN HAIG'S despatches dated 23/5/17	
BOESINGHE	25th		Relieved 15th Welsh Regt in front area BOESINGHE sector. Relief completed 11.30 pm	

Army Form C. 2118.

WAR DIARY
or
INTELLIGENCE SUMMARY.

11th Service Battalion South Wales Borderers (2nd Gwent)

Instructions regarding War Diaries and Intelligence Summaries are contained in F.S. Regs., Part II. and the Staff Manual respectively. Title pages will be prepared in manuscript.

Place	Date	Hour	Summary of Events and Information	Remarks and references to Appendices
BOESINGHE	1917 MAY 28th		Dispositions FRONT LINE – A Coy right; D Coy left; B Coy in Support – VILLAGE ST; C Coy in BOESINGHE CHATEAU GROUNDS.	
"	29th		GOC 115th Brigade visited line	
"	30th		" " " Capt Hogan attended Tents Demonstration.	
"	31st		Relieved by 16th Welch Regt. Relief completed at	

Army Form C. 2118.

WAR DIARY
or
INTELLIGENCE SUMMARY.
(Erase heading not required.)

11th Bn (S) S.W.B. [?]

17.V.
13 sheets

Place	Date	Hour	Summary of Events and Information	Remarks and references to Appendices
	JUNE 1st		Strength of Battalion. Roll of Officers. Lt Col A.D. Reeves Major Sir P. O'Reilly not. R.W.F Capt J.D. Morgan " H.J. Williams " G.E.O. Jenkins " M.E.S. Davies Lt P.W. Loyd " J. Harris " M.B.A. Watkins " J. Richards " E.L. Taylor " O.B. Jones atd. 2nd Lt P. Phillips atd " H.J. Whyte atd 1st S.W.B. Commanding Officer R.W.F. 2nd in command 11th S.W.B. O.C. O Coy " O.C. A Coy " O.C. B Coy " O.C. C Coy " O.C. D Coy Adjutant [signature] Medical Officer 3rd S.W.B. 2nd S.W.B. Transport Officer	

Army Form C. 2118.

WAR DIARY
or
INTELLIGENCE SUMMARY.
(Erase heading not required.)

Instructions regarding War Diaries and Intelligence Summaries are contained in F. S. Regs., Part II. and the Staff Manual respectively. Title pages will be prepared in manuscript.

Place	Date	Hour	Summary of Events and Information	Remarks and references to Appendices
			2nd Lt. L.R. Jones 4.5.R.B.	
			H.C. Ellis	
			L. Lloyd acting 2.m.	
			W.L. Williams	
			F.R. Pembridge	
			G.N.H. Orderly Officer	
			J.H. Bryant Signalling Officer + Mess President	
			E.J. Bullock	
			W.J. Davies	
			H.J. Hutchins	
			J.H. Williams	
			H.O. Jones	
			L. Shaw	
			G. Edwards	
			Capt. E. Evans M.D. R.A.M.C. M. Officer	
			Rev. A.H. Jones C.F. Chaplain	
			Lt. D.E. Evans R.E. i/c R.E.	

WAR DIARY
or
INTELLIGENCE SUMMARY

Army Form C. 2118.

Place	Date	Hour	Summary of Events and Information	Remarks and references to Appendices
	JUNE			
Support trenches 2nd DESINGHE SECTOR	1st		Officers 28 Warrant Officers 6 Sgts. 42 Cpls. 39 L/Cpls. 50 Ors. 521 Total 657	
	2nd		Brig Genl A Marshall 2nd in Cmd 115th Inf Bde was wounded at ELVERDINGHE during an artillery duel. Lt Col A.G. Kalliu assumed temporary command of 115th Inf Bde. Lt Col A Murphy 2nd i/c 16th ME Imperiale assumed 2nd i/c Brigade. Lt Col A.G. Kalliu resumed command of 11th S.W.B.	
	5th		Acting Brigadier held a conference of C.O.s at DLEUST FM at which the return to be taken in case the enemy assumed relief from the Bn. posn was discussed.	

Army Form C. 2118.

WAR DIARY or INTELLIGENCE SUMMARY.

Army Form C. 2118.

(Erase heading not required.)

Place	Date	Hour	Summary of Events and Information	Remarks and references to Appendices
	June 6th		H.M. The Queen of the Belgians presented a box of cigarettes to the Batt: in commemoration of the visit of the King of the Belgians to the front trenches the previous day. Casualties 1st - 6th incl. (incl.) Killed 1, wounded 5. The Batt: relieved the 1st Batt: Welch Reg: in the front line trenches left C Coy right B Coy - Support Coy Village Street, D Coy, Reserve Coy. BOESINGHE SECTOR - Disposition - two line left C Coy right B Coy - Support Coy Village Street, D Coy, Reserve Coy BOESINGHE REDOUBT. H.Q. the trench.	Appendix No.1
Front line BOESINGHE SECTOR	10th		Brig. Gen. J.G. Blake D.S.O. assumed command of 117th Inf. Bde. Major E.W.P. O'Kelly was placed in charge of the 1st Batt: Return Showing Strength - Men of Officers present of units - see appendix No.2.	
	12th		Sent to England. The Batt: was relieved by 12th Notts & Derby in the trenches & moved into Brie Huyset huts at CADZOEN Tm the relief of 12th Notts R.N.F. - Casualties 7th-12th incl. killed Men -2.	Appendix No.2

Army Form C. 2118.

WAR DIARY
or
INTELLIGENCE SUMMARY.
(Erase heading not required.)

Place	Date	Hour	Summary of Events and Information	Remarks and references to Appendices
	JUNE 12th		wounded. Appx 2. Appx 3. Appx 15.	
McOWEN FM	13th		hostile patrol — Very much increased movement of ENEEDINGHE — Major B. R. O'Reilly resumed duties of 2nd in command. Mar. was relieved by the 38th Battalion & proceeded moved to PROVEN where it went under canvas in Central Camp.	Appendix No. 3
PROVEN.	14th		School of Instruction. The Bng. fired enemy 115th Inf Bde. with a entrance at Bde H? at ELVERDINGHE & O.B. Lietspieden gave an outline of measures which would be taken out in the event of hostilities in the near future. The 38th Division being attached to XI Corps. Between the following Divisions; Guards Divn NW of Vlamh through ESSEN FM and a point about 600 yards FM Up Proenbeys Farm. N & a point about 600 yards NW of Vlamh N of IRON CROSS 3rd 39th Divisions will attack tonight. The Guards Division will cooperate on the left and Divisions troops further back	

2353 Wt. W2544/1454 700,000 5/15 D.D.& L.   A.D.S.S./Forms/C. 2118.

WAR DIARY
INTELLIGENCE SUMMARY

Place: PROVEN.

17th.
so far so YET SDS - The 38th Division with H. Arters will 2 Divs to the front line i.e. 114th/115th Bde on the right 113th Bde on the left to have objectives. May the Pilkem Ridge — the 2nd day that the 115th Bde will continue to attack and secure objects beyond the trench again beyond. Entrenching tools not mentioned to be taken. The Divl HdQtrs were permitted themselves of any mark on the Canal Bank.
A video but H.Q.O.C. of the Bdes you are attached to is received. Whichever Bn belongs to the 5th Corps although no orders to this effect have practised. In the meantime I am assumed that the 5th Corps forms part of the Fifth Army. A party trotting party — from Bdes O'Rielly to march over and left by two of the general to Dawson's corner where they march to Thomas at OVER EM.

18th.
took on August in Boesel March and Dickerbush rear of 6 Divers. Awaken returning at 3 a.m.

Army Form C. 2118.

WAR DIARY
or
INTELLIGENCE SUMMARY
(Erase heading not required.)

Instructions regarding War Diaries and Intelligence Summaries are contained in F.S. Regs., Part II. and the Staff Manual respectively. Title Pages will be prepared in manuscript.

Place	Date	Hour	Summary of Events and Information	Remarks and references to Appendices
	19th		Battn. was relieved by 11th Welch — Battn. left Burgomme about 1 A.M. & marched to ELVERDINGHE — via DAWSON'S CORNER — where they entrained at 3 A.M. and arrived at PROVEN about 4.30 A.M. Battn. working party — 3 Col. A & 4 ladies in command — proceeded to RIVOLI FM. Billeted at PROVEN at 9 P.M. & moved from ELVERDINGHE via DAWSON'S CORNER.	
	20th		Relieved by 16th Welch — left Burgomme at 10 A.M. & marched to ELVERDINGHE (entraining point) via LUNAVILLE FM, HUNTER ST. & track. As the entraining place was shelled the Battn. 1½ mile detour through dark & commenced move ∧ 2 miles along the line and commenced move.	
	22nd		Battn. working party — Major E.M.P.O. Kelly in command — proceeded to RIVOLI FM	
	23rd		Battn. relieved by 16th Welch — arrived PROVEN 12.30 A.M.	
	24th		Gen. Sir A. M. La P. Gough K.C.B. Cmdg. 5th Army inspected the men and passed through the camp. — Major J.P. Horsman returned from leave & resumed command of "D" Coy. A draft of 39 N.C.O.s & men joined the Battn. from the Reinforcement Camp.	

WAR DIARY or INTELLIGENCE SUMMARY

Army Form C. 2118.

Place	Date	Hour	Summary of Events and Information	Remarks and references to Appendices
PROVEN	JUNE 23rd		A draft of HQ NCOs who joined the Batt'n from the re-inforcement camp. Brig Gen Crichton Army D.Q.G.S. XV Corps accompanied by HH the Prince of Wales visited the camp. Enormous party - horse jumping match & concours - proceeded to Rivals Fm. Entraining at 9 p.m.	
	24th		Batt'n unit party returned at 4 a.m. Casualties 13th - 23rd incl. 2nd Lt. T.H. Inds wounded. Sgts 1. Ptes 3. wounded. The Btn left PROVEN by bus at 9 a.m. proceeded via H'tou & STEENVOORDE to CASTRE arriving about 1 p.m. Batt'n was billeted in CASTRE	Appendix No. 4.
	25th		Left CASTRE at 8.30 a.m. by bus and proceeded by HAZEBROUCK & AIRE & HESTREHEM arriving at 12 noon. Batt'n was billeted in HESTREHEM. Div H.Q. was at LAIRE.	Appendix No. 5.

A. Caulier
Lt Col. W. Som. B.
Comdg. W. Som. B.

Army Form C. 2118.

WAR DIARY
or
INTELLIGENCE SUMMARY.
(Erase heading not required.)

1917

Army Form C. 2118.

WAR DIARY
or
INTELLIGENCE SUMMARY.
(Erase heading not required.)

Place	Date	Hour	Summary of Events and Information	Remarks and references to Appendices
	July		2nd Lt C. Head — 11th S.W.B — Missing officer Lyngyart C.J. Buttle J.A. Davies W.J. Humphries A.J. Lewis — Missing officer's acct. adj. D.R. Matthews asst J.E. Williams — C.n.F. C.E. Avery — 11th S.W.B. G. Andrews H.J. Roberts — Officers Warrant Officers — 25 Sgts — 6 Cpls — 37 L/Cpls — 34 Ptes — 27 635 Total — 769	

WAR DIARY or INTELLIGENCE SUMMARY

Army Form C. 2118.

Place	Date	Hour	Summary of Events and Information	Remarks and references to Appendices
WESTREHEM	JULY 3rd	9.30 a.m.	The Battn. marched to the ENQUINEGATTE area, 5½ miles NE of WESTREHEM and marked out trenches for practice operations — a complete replica of the hostile trenches opposite the LANCASHIRE FARM SECTOR to being traced out in the above area (R.17), facing SE. — Companies marched back independently as soon as their task was finished.	THE ROVANE ref. att.
	4th	8.30 a.m.	½ Batt. of 1 NCO + 15 files joined the Battn. from the reinforcement camp	
		2.30–5 p.m.	The Battn. marched to the ENQUINEGATTE area	
			The area R.9.b + d was allotted to the Battn. & it carried out Platoon training at Cg a.83. Battn. area	
	5th	5 p.m. 3 a.m.	The Battn. bivouacked at Cg a.83 Battn. area Company training.	
	6th	9.30 a.m. 6 a.m.	Coys marched to billets at WESTREHEM independently. The Battn. marched to the ENQUINEGATTE area where the 115 Inf. Bde. relieved part of us & all in the having "Reserve" the Bde. role to advance in rear of the 113 & 114 Inf. Bdes. with	

Army Form C. 2118.

WAR DIARY
or
INTELLIGENCE SUMMARY.
(Erase heading not required.)

Instructions regarding War Diaries and Intelligence Summaries are contained in F. S. Regs., Part II. and the Staff Manual respectively. Title pages will be prepared in manuscript.

Place	Date	Hour	Summary of Events and Information	Remarks and references to Appendices
WESTREHEM	JULY 6th		The 11th SnD on the right supported by the 10th SnD and the 17th KRF on the left supported by the 18th Welsh when the Landing Brgde. have captured their objective — the Green Line — the 115th Inf. Bde. will push through them. The 9th SnD and 19th KRF will capture the line of the STEEN BEEK from bridgeheads and endeavour, the Divl. Cavalry will then go forward to reconnoitre and as soon as LANGEMARCK is found to be clear the 10th SnD & 17th KRF will move forward and occupy every line made good by the Cavalry.	
		6.30am	The above was carried out as far as the recapturing of the STEEN BEEK. The Batt. advanced by its left enspearing to the movements of the 19th Cnf. which moved with its left on the BUESINGHE – LANGEMARK RAILWAY. The Batt: advanced in rolling formation of Rover columns — Coy on the right supported by B Coy and C Coy on the left supported by D Coy. On reaching the 1000 cross stramps	

Army Form C. 2118.

WAR DIARY
or
INTELLIGENCE SUMMARY.
(Erase heading not required.)

Instructions regarding War Diaries and Intelligence Summaries are contained in F. S. Regs., Part II. and the Staff Manual respectively. Title pages will be prepared in manuscript.

Place	Date	Hour	Summary of Events and Information	Remarks and references to Appendices
	JULY 6th		Broke up into sections/columns. After crossing the Green line the Batt. adopted fighting formation. On reaching the STEENBEEK (any beyond the stream not found) a bridgehead threw out Anti Aircraft Sent A out up in line with Regt. the whole Batt. extended - C Coy across the STEENBEEK as a Bridgehead. A & D Coys in support on this side the STEENBEEK + B Coy in Batt reserve	
		2 pm	The Batt. things went through to an end - the hostile batt. to march and returned back to bivouac.	
	7th	6:00am	The Batt. marched to the ENDUINNE GATE area where the 115 & 2nd K.R. carried out the same scheme as on the 6th inst. Major B de P.O.Kelly proceeded to England to attend the C.O's course at ALDERSHOT. Major G. St J. Morden has assumed acting 2nd in command	
	8th		Lt. R. Carr joined the Battn. from [illegible] reverts to duties of Regt. Q.M.	

Army Form C. 2118.

WAR DIARY
or
INTELLIGENCE SUMMARY.
(Erase heading not required.)

Place	Date	Hour	Summary of Events and Information	Remarks and references to Appendices
WESTROOSEBEKE	JULY 12th		The 38th Welsh Divn carried out a rehearsal of the forthcoming operations on the ENQUINEGATE area, zero hour being 9 a.m.	
		9 a.m.	The 115th Inf Bde went in position on the CANAL BANK having previously assembled at M.25 A.4.5. (Herringbone hrs). The 113th Inf Bde. preceded the 115th Inf Bde. ahead on the 6th inst. The 115th Inf. Bde. advanced in the same order as on the 6th inst. The 11th SwB arrived out the same scheme as had been practised under the average movements except that the Battn advanced in 3 lines instead of 2. A&C Coy in front line, D Coy in second line & B Coy - who carried up consolidating material - in third line.	
		with	Platoons eased the Battn. proceeded in rqd.	
		6.30 p.m.	The Brig Gen Cmdg 115 Inf Bde held a conference at IRON CROSS (Having thus of all officers he explained the days operations and explained more to be carried out on the following day.	
	13th	1.30 a.m.	The Battn in position on the STEENBEEK was relieved by the 10th SwB on relief occupied the GREEN LINE. At 3.20 a.m. the 10th SwB on	

WAR DIARY
or
INTELLIGENCE SUMMARY.
(Erase heading not required.)

Army Form C. 2118.

Place	Date	Hour	Summary of Events and Information	Remarks and references to Appendices
WESTREHEM	JULY 13th		The right supported by the 11th S.W.B. and the 16th Welch on the left supported by the 19th R.W.F. moved forward and attacked LANCEMARCK after the capture of which the 19th R.W.F. delivered a decisive counter-attack on the left.	
		5:30am	Operations ceased. Troops had breakfast.	
		4am	The Brig Gen. cmdg 113th Inf Bde held a conference. Staff officers & officers of the other 3 Bns addressed the BDE on parade referring to their having in this area. Bath: bns marched back to billets.	
			2nd Lt. J. Telfer - Beckford Repl. Territorials joined and posted to C. Coy.	
	14th		Lt. Col. T.H. Smith DSO. 16th Welch - assumed temporary command of the BDE in absence of Brig Gen. H.G. Pope DSO. CMG.	
	16th		The BDE left the LAWE'S area and commenced the march to the FORWARD area. Bn HQrs moved independently according to time-table in order as described below.	

Army Form C. 2118.

WAR DIARY
or
INTELLIGENCE SUMMARY.
(Erase heading not required.)

Instructions regarding War Diaries and Intelligence Summaries are contained in F. S. Regs., Part II. and the Staff Manual respectively. Title pages will be prepared in manuscript.

Place	Date	Hour	Summary of Events and Information	Remarks and references to Appendices
	JULY			
	16th	7.30am	The Batt. marched via ST HILAIRE and HAVERSKIRQUE to GUARBECQUE – 9 miles.	
GUARBECQUE		11.30am	Reached GUARBECQUE and billeted.	
	17th	6.45am	The Batt. marched via THIENNES and HAZEBROUCK to PRADELLES – 16 miles.	
PRADELLES		2.15pm	Billeted in PRADELLES 9 miles to the North.	
	18th	9.a.m.	The Batt. marched to STEENVOORDE a distance of 8 miles	
STEENVOORDE		11.a.m	Arrived at STEENVOORDE where Batt. was billeted in farms south of the town.	
	19th	5.15pm	The Batt. marched to PROVEN via – SMULTS – via WATOU.	
PROVEN		6.30 pm	Batt. reached camp about E.12.c.0.1 (Sheet 2-) Lt. Col. Smyles took over Infantry command a/c 115 Inf. Bde. Lt. R.D. Rolands from 5th Army Musketry School TACQUES and 2nd Lt. R.L. WATTS from our lines reported for duty were posted to H.W.	
	20th		Brig.Gen. Gwynn Thomas DSO R.E took over command of the 115th Inf Bde at a conference at G.O.S 2nd in Command at Ble. H2. Orders issued for the evening Manouvers were received	

Army Form C. 2118.

WAR DIARY
or
INTELLIGENCE SUMMARY

(Erase heading not required.)

Instructions regarding War Diaries and Intelligence Summaries are contained in F. S. Regs., Part II. and the Staff Manual respectively. Title Pages will be prepared in manuscript.

Place	Date	Hour	Summary of Events and Information	Remarks and references to Appendices
PROVEN AREA.	JULY 20th	4pm	The Batt'n marched to the Nr.SIXTE 'S' Area and bivouaced in STAINES CAMP — F.5.B.9.b. Time of arrival 6 p.m. and distance marched 5 miles.	
ST.SIXTE AREA	21st	9.30 am.	The Officers and most N.C.O's of the Batt'n saw the sand model of the enemy's trenches etc. over which we are going to attack. 2nd Lt. J.R. Williams left the Batt'n to proceed to the base. He is medically unfit for the forward area.	
	22nd		A working party of 6 officers and 200 O.R., found by A and B Co's was taken by busses to PARROY F.4. to bury cable.	
		7pm.	The Batteries near were shelled with gas shells and the party worked with their box respirators on for most of the time. Four men only suffered very slightly from the effects of the gas.	
	23rd	4.30 pm	The working party returned to camp by buses.	
		5pm	The C.O. held a conference of company commanders during which the action to be taken on reaching the STEEN BEEK was discussed.	

Army Form C. 2118.

WAR DIARY
or
INTELLIGENCE SUMMARY.
(Erase heading not required.)

Instructions regarding War Diaries and Intelligence Summaries are contained in F.S. Regs., Part II. and the Staff Manual respectively. Title pages will be prepared in manuscript.

Place	Date	Hour	Summary of Events and Information	Remarks and references to Appendices
	JULY			
ST SIXTE AREA	28th	2 pm	Orders were received from 115 Inf. Bde. that the Batt" must be prepared to move at an hours notice.	
		6 pm	Further orders were received for the Batt" stand to until 11.30 p.m. when the previous order "to be ready to move at an hours notice" came into force again.	
		11.30 pm		
	29th	3.30 pm	Brig. Gen. Sir m. Thomas D.S.O. 115 Inf. Bde. addressed the Batt" at 3.30 p.m. He laid stress on the rather of the rifle in modern warfare, and wished the Batt" success in the forthcoming operations.	
		9.30 pm	The B" moved from the corps Mayurs Area to the corps concentration area. The B" marched off at 9.30 pm and arrived at DUBLIN camp at 2.30 am. There the men were billetted for the night in huts.	
DUBLIN CAMP	30th	2.30 am		
			During the day final preparations for equipping the battalion for the attack were made. The Batt" marched from DUBLIN camp to the assembly point - starting at 9.30 p.m. and arrived at 2.30 a.m.	
	31st	9.30 pm 2.30 am		

T2134. Wt. W708—776. 500000. 4/15. Sir J. C. & S.

Army Form C. 2118.

WAR DIARY
or
INTELLIGENCE SUMMARY.
(Erase heading not required.)

Instructions regarding War Diaries and Intelligence Summaries are contained in F.S. Regs., Part II. and the Staff Manual respectively. Title pages will be prepared in manuscript.

Place	Date	Hour	Summary of Events and Information	Remarks and references to Appendices
CANAL BANK.	JULY 31st	2.30 a.m.	The operation orders were carried out with the exception of the modifications contained in the following narrative. The assemble positions were as follows. Bn. H.Q, A & C. Coys were on the CANAL BANK North of Bridge 6a, B" H.Q. being located at GRAY'S INN. Two sections of the 115. M.G.C. and 115 T.M. Bty. were also with Bn. H.Q. B. 90. Coys were assembled at HUGH'S FARM C.18.b.9.9. (Sheet 28.N.W. 2). July 31st being Z day and zero hour 3.50 a.m. and the battⁿ due to start off at zero + 1. H.O, the leading Coys. were clear of the CANAL by 5.30 a.m. The only casualties caused whilst the Bn was clearing the canal were incurred by B" H.Q. when 10. O.R. were wounded during the crossing of Bridge 6A. No great opposition was met by the 113 and 114 Bdes except in CANDLE TRENCH, until after the Black line was passed, so that the Bⁿ was able to keep to the time table laid down, and prisoners began to come back freely.	11 *S.W.B. Lieut. 43 by Lt. Col. A.H. Radice attached
		6.50 a.m.	As the attacking troops neared the green line, they experienced machine gun and rifle fire from concrete dugouts and gun emplacements and several casualties were caused. Capt C.F.R. Jenkins O/C. C. Coy and	

WAR DIARY
or
INTELLIGENCE SUMMARY.
(Erase heading not required.)

Army Form C. 2118.

Place	Date	Hour	Summary of Events and Information	Remarks and references to Appendices
GREEN LINE	JULY 31st		Lt. R.V. Sayer were both wounded by bullets, before the green line was reached. The green line was successfully taken by the 14th Bn. Welsh Regt. and the Bn. then passed through them, and getting into attack formation pushed forward towards the STEENBEKE. Considerable opposition was met from m.g. and rifle fire, but all opposition was overcome and the points mopped up. The enemy were quickly cleared from the STEENBEKE itself. A Coys then pushed across the STEENBEKE and establishes the bridge head at AU BON GITE Coy and Two Platoons of A Coy proceeded to consolidate their position under m.g. fire from LANGEMARCK. Snipers were also very active. Owing to the obstruction of the cable head by shell fire, communication with the rear was very difficult and the German shelled heavily behind our positions. Just after our positions were reached four German aeroplanes flew over our line from the direction of LANGEMARK and dropped bombs and fired m.g.s on our garrison. A gun was also seen in LANGEMARK very limbered up and taken away	

Army Form C. 2118.

WAR DIARY
or
INTELLIGENCE SUMMARY.
(Erase heading not required.)

Place	Date	Hour	Summary of Events and Information	Remarks and references to Appendices
ST GEORGES	JULY 31st	3 pm	**Infantry** — Two Battns of Germans were seen marching through LANGEMARCK to counter attack. An S.O.S. was sent up but was answered by artillery, but the attack was repulsed by Lewis, machine gun & rifle fire. On our left however the 17th R.W.F. withdrew their trench. The STEENBEEK leaving our left flank exposed. A more vigorous attack was then made and some concrete buildings on our left flank were seized by the enemy. 7 M.G. from this position made our line over the Steen untenable, so that our line was withdrawn to the banks of the river. The Germans then tried to secure the bridge head but failed.	
		4 pm	The artillery on both sides proceeded to register. The enemy soon began to bring accurate fire to bear on our trenches and many casualties were caused. About this time both Lt Colonel At Radice and 2nd Lt. L. Lloyd (Signalling Offr) were badly wounded by a shell at Bn H.Q. Capt. B.E.S. Davis ⟨?/Adjt⟩ took over command of the Bn. at 9 pm.	To the North of the Steenbeke
		8.30 pm	The Germans were seen massing in shell holes in front of LANGEMARCK and they attacked the sun banks under cover of heavy artillery	

Army Form C. 2118.

WAR DIARY
or
INTELLIGENCE SUMMARY.

(Erase heading not required.)

Place	Date	Hour	Summary of Events and Information	Remarks and references to Appendices
STEENBECK	JULY 31st	8.30 PM	Our S.O.S. was quickly answered by the artillery who brought the barrage down on the attacking troops and caused very many casualties. The Vickers gunners did very effective work. The attack failed, and during the night the artillery fire on both sides was fairly heavy. The following officers were casualties during the operation. 2nd Lt. R.C. Green. E. Coy. killed 2nd Lt. H. Roberts. O Coy. wounded 2nd Lt. G.F. Bullock D Coy. killed 2nd Lt. D.G. Humphries C Coy. wounded 2nd Lt. T.G. Williams A Coy. wounded Capt. E. Evans. R.A.M.C. wounded 2nd Lt. L.M. Mathews B Coy. wounded Lt Col. Applebee. O.C. wounded S.O. wounded (shell pieces) 2/Lt. L. Lloyd.	

Signed M. Llewelyn Copp
A/Lt Col
Commanding 11 SWB

115/38

Army Form C. 2118.

WAR DIARY
or
INTELLIGENCE SUMMARY
(Erase heading not required.)

19.V.
17 sheets

Place	Date	Hour	Summary of Events and Information	Remarks and references to Appendices
STEENBEEK U22 C 2 U28 d 33	1917 Aug 1st	2 AM	The weather turned out not favorable as all day there was rain. Rations and small parties were very difficult during the morning, the situation by the STEENBEEK was not at all clear as troops & supply dropping and M.G. fire made all communication difficult.	

WAR DIARY
or
INTELLIGENCE SUMMARY.
(Erase heading not required.)

Army Form C. 2118.

Place	Date	Hour	Summary of Events and Information	Remarks and references to Appendices
STEENBECK	Aug 10 (cont.)	11 am	Orders were received from 115 Inf Bde that the 13th was to cross the STEENBECK and form a Bridge head again at AUBOY GITE. 2nd LT. G WATTS was sent forward with the order to the senior officer in charge of the line and also to endeavour to find what was happening. LT B. H. JONES of B Coy was in charge, with 2nd LT. VIZER with D Coy & 2nd LT. TRELOAR with about 30 men of C. Coy. No information could be obtained as to the situation right of the PILCKEM - LANGEMARKE ROAD. Provisional arrangements were made to attack in conjunction with the artillery and 115 M.G.C. at 1.30 pm	
		12.10 am	The Bde. Major and Capt. B.E.S. Davies moved forward from B. H. Q. to the right flank to find A. Coy and also to supervise and make to ascertain if an attack was possible. Just short of the STEENBECK, Capt. Davies was killed by a sniper, the Bde Capt Harris over command	
		1 pm	Major cancelled the attack owing to the situation. O.k.B.	
		3 pm	The GERMANS opened a very heavy artillery fire on the STEENBECK position and on B. H. Q. Also all roads and tracks and	

WAR DIARY
or
INTELLIGENCE SUMMARY.

(Erase heading not required.)

Army Form C. 2118.

Place	Date Aug	Hour	Summary of Events and Information	Remarks and references to Appendices
STEENBECK	1 (cont)		possible lines of approach from Bde H.q. to Bn. H.q. and to the STEEN BECK.	
		6pm	This fire became so heavy that the line withdrew about 250 yards and took up a fresh position in shell holes in the northward. Lt. B.H. Jones was wounded. At dusk the original line was	
		9pm	reoccupied although the shelling was still very severe. 2nd/Lt M.W. Lancaster with a patrol of four men endeavoured to get into touch with the left of the division to our right, without result.	
		11pm	2nd/Lt. M.W. Lancaster with 1 Platoon of B. Company was sent to strengthen the line. Throughout the night the shelling did not slacken, and at times became very intense. No communication by telephone could be maintained, and communication by runner was the only link to Bde & to the front line. The runners and signallers suffered heavily during this shelling, and B. Coy 178. H.q. also.	

WAR DIARY or INTELLIGENCE SUMMARY

Army Form C. 2118.

Place	Date	Hour	Summary of Events and Information	Remarks and references to Appendices
STEENBECK	Oct 2nd	12.1am	Orders were received from Bde that the Bn would be relieved by the 13th Bn. Royal Welsh Fusiliers and also the 9th Welsh Regt. The relief of the B was arranged as follows:- the 13th be would proceed to the support area with H.Q. at MAUSER COT and strong points at C.8.a.6.2 C.14.a.5.9 GALWITZ Fm. & CHEMIN DRIVE. C.2.c.9.4. the remainder of the Bn. to stand fast in CHEMIN DRIVE to reinforce the BLACK LINE. The Bn. H.Q. of the 13th Royal Welsh Fusiliers were situated in STAY Fm. C.3.c.27. This Battn. was ordered to occupy a line and consolidate it about 250x South of the STEENBECK, so that the companies on the STEENBECK were not relieved.	
MAUSER COT C.14.a.5.9.		5 am 6 pm	B H.Q. and 1 Platoon of B. Company left the STEENBECK position and arrived at MAUSER COT Gm. Owing to the extreme difficulty of the first relief and the shortage of men, the relief was not complete until 8.p.m.	
		9am	Major G.J. Monteith arrived and took over command of the Battn. from Capt. Harris who had been O.C. and Adjutant since Capt. B.S. Davis' death	

WAR DIARY
or
INTELLIGENCE SUMMARY.
(Erase heading not required.)

Army Form C. 2118.

Place	Date	Hour	Summary of Events and Information	Remarks and references to Appendices
SUPPORT AREA	Aug 2nd cont.	6pm	A ration party from CHEMIN DRIVE was sent to PILCKEM CROSS ROADS and during the journey suffered seven casualties - 2 killed and 5 wounded. During the whole of the day the weather was bad, rain falling heavily the whole time. During the night Mr LANCASTER'S Platoon of B Coy and A Coy were relieved on the STEEN BECK. A Coy it appears had withdrawn 200° S of the STEEN BECK under cover of a hedge. LT. WHYTE and 2ND LT. W.J. ROBERTS were the Officers left with the company. On relief they proceeded to CORRIDOR TR. and the dugouts and trenches in FARGATE.	
E. CANAL BANK, N of SWAAN HOFF FM. C.18.b.53	Aug 3rd	5 AM	In the area N of SWAAN HOFF FM, on the E. Bank of the canal. The Brigadier Gen. Cmg 115 Inf Bde. visited the battn about 5am. He went round the different strong points and posts conversing with the men on the previous operation.	
		11:30am	The rest of the bn. to left the MOUSER COT area for FARGATE at 17.30 am. There was no regular relief owing to the	

WAR DIARY
or
INTELLIGENCE SUMMARY.

(Erase heading not required.)

Army Form C. 2118.

Place	Date	Hour	Summary of Events and Information	Remarks and references to Appendices
CANAL BANK.	Aug 3rd		dispositions of Battalions being altered	
		1.30pm	Relief completed.	
			During the remainder of the day the Battn rested and started reorganizing in case that it should be required suddenly.	
		10pm	The Bn was ordered to "Stand to"	
			During the night C Coy were relieved on the STEENBECK and	
		6am	arrived on the CANAL BANK at 6 am	
			During the day the Battn continued its work of reorganizing.	
	Aug 5.	12.4pm	The Battn was relieved at noon by a Battn of the Duke of Cornwall's Light Infantry belonging to the 20th Div. The Battn	
ELVERDINGHE.			then marched to ELVERDINGHE CHATEAU GROUNDS. Here the Battn was served with hot food, clean socks provided. Twelve men, feet tender. Twelve cases of sickness and bad feet were evacuated to the Field Ambulance.	
ST. SIXTE.		5.30 pm	The Battn marched to ELVERDINGHE St" and entrained and proceeded to INTERNATIONAL CORNER St" near ST. SIXTE	

WAR DIARY
or
INTELLIGENCE SUMMARY

Army Form C. 2118.

Place	Date	Hour	Summary of Events and Information	Remarks and references to Appendices
ST. SIXTE.	Aug 5th	7/45 p.m.	After detraining the Batt. marched to STAYNES CAMP and bivouced there to reequipment. The total casualties during these operations numbered 330 killed, wounded missing.	

Army Form C. 2118.

WAR DIARY
or
INTELLIGENCE SUMMARY.
(Erase heading not required.)

Instructions regarding War Diaries and Intelligence Summaries are contained in F. S. Regs., Part II. and the Staff Manual respectively. Title pages will be prepared in manuscript.

Place	Date	Hour	Summary of Events and Information	Remarks and references to Appendices
STAIVES	1917 AUG. 6		Resting all day. MAJ. JR ANGUS. LIEUTEN. RLEE. ETAR our command and 2/LT COOK.	
	7	1PM	Draft of 102 OR. Nat. PHILLIPS & CAPT PAGE arrived. Day was spent in re-forming and re-equipping the Batt. and teaching the Lewisonal Commander. Major Blackader and Lieut Commander Lieut Cowan visited the Batt. in the afternoon and L/Cowan thro Phillips in the work the Batt. had just done in the attack	
	8		Training in the morning. Inspection by Brig. Gen. GWYN THOMAS in the afternoon, who told the officers particular points to be observed in the next attack. 2/Lt TEFFCOTT reported Re-organising Companies	
	9		Training in morning. Baths at CHATEAU COUTHEAU in afternoon	
	10		Two two building range all day on TRAINING AREA. Remainder training in the morning & football & cross-country running in the afternoon. RANGE completed at 2.15 PM	
	11		Morning Church parade. LEWIS GUN firing LT. EDY PHILLIPS proceeded to town as permanent instrt. for troops in town and new Draft 34 OR arrived	
	12			
	13		Training & firing on new Range all day.	
	14		Training	
	15		as Henry return interpined in afternoon	

Army Form C. 2118.

WAR DIARY
or
INTELLIGENCE SUMMARY.
(Erase heading not required.)

Instructions regarding War Diaries and Intelligence Summaries are contained in F. S. Regs., Part II. and the Staff Manual respectively. Title pages will be prepared in manuscript.

Place	Date	Hour	Summary of Events and Information	Remarks and references to Appendices
STAINES	1917 AUG 16		Hqrs Runners & Signallers took part in a BRIGADE scheme of visual signalling in the attack. All moving contact planes took part. Remainder of Battn. training and baths at CHATEAU COUTHONE	
	17	9.30 PM	Local action Evening. Bruin received to move to CANAL BANK to morrow.	
			Enemy planes over which dropped bombs in the district. Several bombs dropped on the 10th S.W.B. lines & the HOSPITAL inflicting casualties	
	18	11.45 AM	Battn moved to INTERNATIONAL CORNER under the command of MAJ J.H.MONTEITH	
		1.0 PM	Entrained	B2.c.0.8.8.
		1.30	Detrained at ELVERDINGE and marched to DAWSON'S CORNER where dinner was taken	
		4.15	Arrived at CANAL BANK	
CANAL BANK		8.30	Relief of 19th WELCH complete. Dispositions between Bridges 6x & 6yd 4 & 5 C.13.b.2.3	
		10.30	D.Coy sent out to take positions in shell holes near GLIMPSE COT Enemy shelled	
			CANAL BANK intermittently throughout the night	
	19		Working party of 3 platoons on tramways all day.	
		7.15 PM	Artillery Carrying party of 100 O.R. questioned 30 casualties at CHIEN FARM U.22d.7.8	
			Enemy artillery quiet. Our artillery busy all night.	

Army Form C. 2118.

WAR DIARY
or
INTELLIGENCE SUMMARY.
(Erase heading not required.)

Instructions regarding War Diaries and Intelligence Summaries are contained in F. S. Regs., Part II. and the Staff Manual respectively. Title pages will be prepared in manuscript.

Place	Date	Hour	Summary of Events and Information	Remarks and references to Appendices
CANAL BANK	1917 AUG 20		Lewis gun & training all day	
	21	7:30 AM	Our artillery opened an intense bombardment & Enemy Retired on our right and	
			Kept up a intermittent shelling throughout the day	
		9:30 PM	Enemy put about 15 shells (4.2) on the CANAL under Aug Dyke. No damage	
	22	2 AM	Enemy dropped 4 2" and 9" shells on & around the CANAL	
		4 AM	Our artillery opened heavy bombardment to which lasted till 9am. Several	
			batches of prisoners passed over Bridges 6 during the morning	
		4 PM	8 Enemy planes passed over and dropped bombs on E & W sides of CANAL	
		10:15 PM	Enemy planes over again at great height. Artillery quiet during night	
			Orders received to relieve 13th WELCH in the line	
	23	7:30 PM	Batt'n started to move from CANAL BANK in parties of 25 at 100 yds interval	
		8:30 PM	Front party passed CANDLE TRENCH at C 8 q.8	
LINE U29 a 8.6		11:57 PM	Relief complete. Batt'n HQRS with MAJOR MONTEITH in command are at ALOUETTE FARM. Two Companies (B & D) are in the front line and hold from U29 a 80.70 to U24 c 00.40 (D Coy) and from U24c 00.40 to U30 a 4.9. The supports U29 a 8.6 (A & C Coys) are approx from U29 d 10.55 to U29 b 35.60 and from U29 a 5.90.6	

WAR DIARY
or
INTELLIGENCE SUMMARY.
(Erase heading not required.)

Army Form C. 2118.

Place	Date	Hour	Summary of Events and Information	Remarks and references to Appendices
LINE U29a8.6	1917 AUGUST		U29a 6.5.70. TM 19th RW3 + 6th BEDSR Regt on Sn our left + right respectively. When the Battn was on its way up the SOS was being sent from ALOUETTE FARM by lamp. Shortly after # our artillery opened a very intense bombardment and the signal stop was sent. The enemy barrage just escaped to our casualties coming up were 1 OFFICER wounded.	
	23/24	NIGHT	Artillery of both sides active. The enemy's fixed barrage lines are:— LANGEMARK — POELCAPELLE RD; LANGEMARK — PILKEM RD; LANGEMARK — ALOUETTE FARM RD. Midway between STEENBEEK and LANGEMARK — ALOUETTE FARM RD; STEEN BEEK V13c5.3	
	24	1am	Fire opened about TRAGIQUE FARM which lasted several hours	
		DAWN	Our front line boys with about about 400+ behind their line to prepare for heavy Artillery bombardment. A patrol from our left Coy reported no sign of enemy patrols or working parties but that the enemy had a post at approx U23d 92.60	
		7 pm	Enemy plane flying low driven off by Rate aircraft and Lewis Guns	
		9.25 pm	Front line re-occupied by 2 front Coys	
		11 pm	Artillery of both sides very active	

Army Form C. 2118.

WAR DIARY
or
INTELLIGENCE SUMMARY.
(Erase heading not required.)

Instructions regarding War Diaries and Intelligence Summaries are contained in F.S. Regs., Part II. and the Staff Manual respectively. Title pages will be prepared in manuscript.

Place	Date	Hour	Summary of Events and Information	Remarks and references to Appendices
LINE U29a 8 L	1917 Aug 24	NIGHT	Enemy machine gun appeared to be firing from U23d 80 80 do do at U23d 92 65 & U23d 80 50 believed to be silenced by our guns. Numerous Very lights were put up by the enemy.	
	24	9.5pm	A patrol under 2/Lt PEMBRIDGE found EAGLE TRENCH severely damaged by our artillery & found several enemy dead in the trench and its dug-outs. A new patrol was started from U24 c 30 80 and was fired on & scattered bombing at about the same time.	
	25	5.30AM	Two enemy planes flew over our lines at 5.35 AM & 6.30 PM. About 8 were seen at 8.10AM. Artillery quiet throughout the day. Hostile fellow on Right Divron front unarmed up for an hour. Enemy planes over our lines for nearly an hour. Throughout the night enemy infantry was very quiet. Very lights were put up at intervals from EAGLE TRENCH. Our artillery was active during the night. A patrol secured identification papers & shoulder straps from enemy dead in EAGLE TRENCH.	

Army Form C. 2118.

WAR DIARY
or
INTELLIGENCE SUMMARY.
(Erase heading not required.)

Instructions regarding War Diaries and Intelligence Summaries are contained in F. S. Regs., Part II. and the Staff Manual respectively. Title pages will be prepared in manuscript.

Place	Date	Hour	Summary of Events and Information	Remarks and references to Appendices
LINE U29a.8.6	1917 Aug 26	6AM	Enemy plane brought down in our lines. Jerry MG's at a height of about 200 ft one of these was brought down in our lines by AA fire	
		9.9AM	Enemy plane brought down about U22c Central.	
		2.55pm	Our artillery (heavier - believed 9.2) firing short around U23d.4.1 what was rectified at 3.25pm	
		NIGHT	During the night our artillery carried on an intermittent shelling of enemy lines. Enemy artillery was extremely quiet. The 16th Bn Welch Regt moved up behind our lines to be in readiness for the attack of 27th inst. Enemy infantry & MGs very quiet.	
	27	3.17AM	The enemy shelled this usual barrage line heavily fell down after	
		9AM 1.55PM	which no contact or shelling firing all the morning. One officer & men of R.E. reported to unexpired ALOUETTE FARM until 7.55pm. Our artillery opened very heavy trench-destruct. Enemy responded 2 minutes later i.e. in 10 minutes had a very heavy fire on our naval barrage line. This	
		8.10PM	increased in intensity and obtained its maximum at 35 minutes after ZERO. Enemy putting up white lights	
		8.30PM	Contact plane observed	

Army Form C. 2118.

WAR DIARY
or
INTELLIGENCE SUMMARY.

(Erase heading not required.)

Instructions regarding War Diaries and Intelligence
Summaries are contained in F. S. Regs., Part II.
and the Staff Manual respectively. Title pages
will be prepared in manuscript.

Place	Date	Hour	Summary of Events and Information	Remarks and references to Appendices
LINE U29a86	1917 AUG 27	2 PM	The 16th WELCH moved through our front to the attack. They were met by very heavy machine Gun fire and snipers and were unable to take their objectives. One platoon under 2/Lt ROBERTS relief Liaison Platoon between the 16th WELCH and the 6th DUKE of WELLINGTONS on the right. WHITE HOUSE 5.10 U24c5.10 was taken by the 6th D of W and 2 sections of our platoon were left under Mr ROBERTS at WHITE HOUSE till 10 P.M. U24c5.10	
		5 PM	Enemy barrage died down to desultory firing	
		5.15	Our barrage ceased	
		6.55"	Our artillery opened another barrage on the right which lasted for 1 hour. The enemy replied immediately and put up an intense barrage. Heavy barrage until 10 P.M.	
		NIGHT	The 16 Welch were withdrawn and a Coy of the 10th SWB were sent up and took positions from approx. U23d5.36 U23d63.10. Enemy artillery quiet	
	28		Enemy artillery abnormally quiet. Our artillery fairly active Wind too strong for aircraft	

(A5783) Wt. W8079/M1072 350,000 4/17 Sch. 52a Forms/C2118/14
D. B. & L., London, E.C.

WAR DIARY
or
INTELLIGENCE SUMMARY.
(Erase heading not required.)

Army Form C. 2118.

Place	Date	Hour	Summary of Events and Information	Remarks and references to Appendices
LINE	1917 AUG 28	PM 2.50	Our heavy firing shot & inflicting casualties on our Right Bn	
U29aS.6	29	AM 2.15	After a quiet night enemy shelled our support areas till dawn - after that it was quiet. The MG's + snipers were firing only slightly below throughout the night 28/29.	
		3 PM	Bombing Patrol of 3 enemy approached our lines & but was fired on. Leaving one dead one wounded & prisoner. The latter & POW's were sent to Bde. Boundaries established between my Right Bn & the 6TH YORKS U28c5,10 - U28c7,10	
		AM 12.30	Patrols reported EAGLE TRENCH through WHITE HOUSE but movement & snipers. No movement seen of any kind.	
		PM 11.15	Heard from dug outs in rear. Enemy put over gas shells around LANGEMARK but no casualties. Lots of shrapnel.	
		PM 7.35	Enemy put up flares breaking into a golden spray after which fell 30 mins or so. He put up a heavy barrage on our support area which lasted Showery all day	

WAR DIARY
or
INTELLIGENCE SUMMARY.

(Erase heading not required.)

Army Form C. 2118.

Instructions regarding War Diaries and Intelligence Summaries are contained in F. S. Regs., Part II. and the Staff Manual respectively. Title pages will be prepared in manuscript.

Place	Date	Hour	Summary of Events and Information	Remarks and references to Appendices
LINE	1917 AUG 29	PM 11.30	Relief by 16th R.W.F. started. Incidents very few and no trouble on the	
U29a&6	30	AM 4.30	way to & thousand. Relief complete 2.35 AM 9.30th	
		PM 12.0	Relief of CANDLE TRENCH complete C2d07.08 – C5d98. Complete rest till now – Cleaning up/visits etc.	
		8.30	Working Party of 200 OR or tramways E of STEENBEEK. Two OR wounded	
		8.45	Relief of CANDLE TRENCH by 13th WELCH started, and we moved to	
B23c&4	31	11.30	L2 (LEIPZIG FARM). B23c4.4	
		AM 1.30	Relief of bivouacs complete Working parties returned	
		PM 7.30	Rest all morning – baths at ELVERDINGHE in afternoon. 11 enemy planes over.	

Signed

Major
O.C. 11th Pan [?]

Army Form C. 2118.

WAR DIARY
or
INTELLIGENCE SUMMARY.
(Erase heading not required.)

Instructions regarding War Diaries and Intelligence Summaries are contained in F. S. Regs., Part II. and the Staff Manual respectively. Title pages will be prepared in manuscript.

Place	Date	Hour	Summary of Events and Information	Remarks and references to Appendices
			Roll of Officers August 1917	
			Lt Col J R Angus	
			MAJ J H L MONTEITH	
			„ E D PHILLIPS	
			CAPT I A MORGAN	
			„ W G WILLIAMS	
			„ G D PAGE	
			„ IVT HARRIS	
			LT R J RICHARDS 2/LT E R DENBRIDGE	
			„ W H A WILKINS „ G WARD	
			„ E R TAYLOR	
			„ E D V PHILLIPS „ T H BRYANT	
			„ W J WAYTE „ H W LANCASTER	
			„ I R LLOYD „ S G GRIFFIN	
			„ T H DAVIES „ W J RODERTS	
			„ P J TRELOAR	
			„ E R TEFFCOTT	
			„ H H MORRIS	

WAR DIARY or INTELLIGENCE SUMMARY

Army Form C. 2118.

XI 8 W B Vol 20

20.V.
6 sheets

Place	Date	Hour	Summary of Events and Information	Remarks and references to Appendices
MIHAKOFF FARM AREA	1/9/17		Battalion working party from 9-30 A.M. to 5 P.M. for all ranks employed. Men working on tents near ELVERDINGHE	
	2/9/17		Battalion working party from 9-30 A.M. to 2 P.M. for all ranks employed. Men working on tents near ELVERDINGHE. Enemy fired two shells at 10-45 A.M. in the vicinity of the Camp. At 1-30 P.M. four more shells and at 2-45 P.M. two more shells, the last two being very close to the Camp. Great aerial activity on both sides all evening.	
	3/9/17		Inspection by O.C. at 8.30 A.M. Drawing and firing on Range at B.22.6.8.8. Sheet 28. G.O.C. 115th Infantry Brigade inspected Military Medals 20538/C/16 Maloney P and 24182 Le Evans O at 5.0 P.M. Great aerial activity throughout the day.	
	4/9/17		Training throughout the day. Battalion moved at 6.0 P.M. to	

Army Form C. 2118.

WAR DIARY
or
INTELLIGENCE SUMMARY.
(Erase heading not required.)

Place	Date	Hour	Summary of Events and Information	Remarks and references to Appendices
PROVEN AREA			Entrained 10-30 a.m. Detrained PROVEN 11-20 A.M. Relieved 7th K.O.S.L.I. at E.12.c.17. Palgaola Camp at 12 noon. Below the remainder of the day	
	10/9/17		Training and re-organising during the morning. Baths at CHATEAU COUTHOVE in the afternoon	
	11/9/17		Training all morning. O.C. inspected Battalion by companies in the afternoon	
EECKE AREA	12/9/17		Battalion moved off from PROVEN Camp to EECKE AREA at 7.15 A.M. Arrived 12-30 P.M. Headquarters at Q.19.a.4.8. Sheet 27.	
MORBECQUE AREA	13/9/17		Battalion marched from EECKE Area at 9.30 A.M. to MORBECQUE Area	
ESTAIRES AREA	14/9/17		Battalion marched from MORBECQUE AREA to ESTAIRES AREA at 9.20 A.M. Dinners were served on the road near MERVILLE. Batt: billeted in SAILLY-SUR-LA-LYS for the night	
	15/9/17		Batt: marched from SAILLY at 7.20 P.M. and relieved 2/5th L.N.Lancs in	

WAR DIARY
or
INTELLIGENCE SUMMARY.

Army Form C. 2118.

Place	Date	Hour	Summary of Events and Information	Remarks and references to Appendices
TALANA FARM			TALANA FARM B.1.F.C. 90.93 Sheet 28. Relief Complete 8-45.P.M. Working Party of 5 Officers and 200 O.R. burying Cable from ALOVETTE Fm to MU-RON-GATE One Casualty. Returned at 3-30 a.m. Great aerial activity	
	5/9/17		Battalion working Parti - night wiring from THE ING'S to KT STADEN Railway. Party returned 3-30 a.m.	
	6/9/17		Battalion working Parti on night wiring from THE ING'S to the STADEN Railway Returned 2-45 A.M	
	7/9/17		Battalion working Party except wiring from THE ING'S to the STADEN Railway. Party returned at 3-40 a.m.	
	8/9/17		Battalion Working Party - wiring from THE ING'S to the STADEN Railway Party returned from 2.0. P.M. to 7-30. P.M. Visibility being very poor owing to burst of 2 Officers and 50 O.R. Continued the work from 7-45 p.m. to 1-45 a.m.	
	9/9/17		Battalion moved at 9-15 a.m. from TALANA Fm forward to ELVERDINGHE	

WAR DIARY
or
INTELLIGENCE SUMMARY.

Army Form C. 2118.

Place	Date	Hour	Summary of Events and Information	Remarks and references to Appendices
ARMENTIERES SECTOR			Recce Area ARMENTIERES Section. Relief Complete at 1.0 A.M. on 16/9/17. HQ. and 2 Companies billeted in Lawrence H.52.d.3.5. Sheet 36. Two Companies in the SUBSIDIARY LINE C.22.c.65.10 to E.4.c.51.42 and under Command of 7/10 K.S.L.I. sent to 1st Battalion holding the Front Line.	
	16/9/17		Church parades in AM. morning. Reconnaissance of Roads and positions in Area. Also training in the Afternoon. Aerial activity noted. Sides.	
	17/9/17		Lt Colonel T.R. ANGUS / Wounded whilst talking in 15 L.Y.S. old S.15 A.M. Buried in ERQUINGHEM Cemetery at 3.0 P.M. Same day. All available Officers and Senior NCOs attend.	
	18/9/17		Platoon and Company training & Reconnaissance of Front Line.	
	19/9/17		Platoon and Company training. Reconnaissance of Front Line. Major T.E.C. PARTRIDGE WELCH REGT. arrived and assumed Command of the Battalion	
	20/9/17		Platoon and Company training. Reconnaissance of Front Line and ARMENTIERES Defences.	
	21/9/17		Platoon and Coy. training. 1 Officer and 34 OR. Survey Cable Colonies 3.0 P.M	

WAR DIARY
or
INTELLIGENCE SUMMARY.

(Erase heading not required.)

Army Form C. 2118.

Place	Date	Hour	Summary of Events and Information	Remarks and references to Appendices
ARMENTIERES SECTOR	22/9/17		Platoon and Coy Training — Working Party of 1 Officer & 40 O.R. Carrying Cable. Returned at 2.30 p.m.	
LEPINETTE SUB-SECTOR	23/9/17		Platoon and Coy Training. Rain. Coy came relieves 1/6 Glas'n, of 10th S.W.B. in the Front line – Relief Commencing at 5.30 a.m. Relief Completed by such day.	
	24/9/17		MAJ. J.H.I. MONTEITH Second in Command. Proceeded on leave. Battalion "On Coy" On Coy in Reserve 10 S.W.B in the Front line. A to C Bn Rd Britanic at the Rendezvous moving at 7.30 p.m. ("D" am) 1 + C Coys in Exhibition line also moving forward at 7.30 p.m. Distribution – A Coy on the Right. B Coy in Centre. C Coy on Left. of Front line. D Coy being in Reserve. Relief Completed 10.30 p.m. Our line appears the quiet but is very bright, and a lot of work regime to be done.	
	25/9/17		Quiet day. A hundred of men which left our line at T.S.C. 50 L40 have been taken by the large enemy party which endeavoured to envelope them.	
	26/9/17		Quiet day except for a few M.M.S and T.M.S which did no damage.	

D. D. & L., London, E.C.
(A7883) Wt. W60/M1672 350,000 4/17 **Sch. 32a** Forms C/2118/14

Army Form C. 2118.

WAR DIARY
or
INTELLIGENCE SUMMARY.
(Erase heading not required.)

Place	Date	Hour	Summary of Events and Information	Remarks and references to Appendices
ARMENTIERES SECTOR	28/9/17		Quiet day. Enemy aerial activity. One Enemy plane flying very low and fired into our trenches. He was driven off by L.G. and Rifle fire. (No casualties caused)	
	29/9/17		Enemy shelled our front line with Gas T.M. Bombs during the early morning and again at 7-0 o'clock in the evening. No casualties occurred. Silenced by retaliation from Artillery.	
	30/9/17		Enemy aeroplanes frequently over our lines by day. Artillery of both sides very quiet. Every one was busy with preparation of hostilities of reprisals. No enemy action followed.	

Alfred Cope
Adjutant for Lieut-Colonel
Commanding 11th South Wales Borderers

OCT 2 1917
11TH. SERVICE BATT.
STH. WALES BORDERERS

WAR DIARY or INTELLIGENCE SUMMARY

(Erase heading not required.)

Army Form C. 2118.

21.V.
9 sheets

NOMINAL ROLL OF OFFICERS. — 11TH BATTALION. SOUTH WALES BORDERERS
(Actually with Battalion.)

1-10-17

Lt. Col.	F.C. PARTRIDGE (10TH WELCH REGT.)
Major	C.J. PHILLIPS. — 2/O (SECOND)-IN-COMMAND
Captain	I.A. MORGAN
Captain	W.G. WILLIAMS
Captain	M.G. RICHARDS
Captain	W.T. HARRIS — Adjutant
Captain	C.H. HOFFMEISTER
Lieut.	L.M. DAVIES
+/Captain	MARKHAM. R.A.M.C. (M.O.)
HON. LIEUT & Q.M.	A. COX.
2/Lieut	M.W.H. LANCASTER — ASSISTANT ADJUTANT.
2/Lieut	P.J. TRELOAR.
2/Lieut	W.J. ROBERTS
2/Lieut	S.G. GRIFFIN.
2/Lieut	H.E. GRIFFITHS
2/Lieut	J.H. HALL
2/Lieut	L.A. LOHNON
2/Lieut	D.T. LACEY.

WAR DIARY or INTELLIGENCE SUMMARY

Army Form C. 2118.

11TH SERVICE BATTⁿ
NOV 1 1917
STH. WALES BORDERERS

Place	Date	Hour	Summary of Events and Information	Remarks and references to Appendices
L'EPINETTE	1/10/17		Hostile artillery was more active to-day than for some time but caused no change or casualties	
	2/10/17		Lewis gun teams of the 10th S.W.B. relieved our Lewis gun teams in the front line during the day. Relief complete 4.15 p.m. 10th S.W.B. also Lewis gun relieved 11th S.W.B. in the front line after dark. Relief complete 11.15 p.m. 11th S.W.B. less 2 Coys remaining in Subsidiary Line (A & C Coys) proceeded to billets at "LAUNDRIES" at H5A57 sheet 36.	
LAUNDRIES H5A57 SHEET 36	3/10/17		Baths were allotted for the whole battalion at the Divisional Baths on the 38ª. LAUNDRIES. A & C Coys in SUBSIDIARY LINE were relieved for the purpose of bathing by B & D Coys who had previously had theirs.	
	4/10/17		Working party of 2 Officers & 60 O.R. proceeded to I3 central sheet 36 to report to Major O'Kelly reported the battalion Commanding Officer were attached.	
	5/10/17		4th Batt C.E.P. were attached to us for instruction. Portuguese were being put Factory ARMENTIERES L29b 6.6 sheet 36. Working party of 1 Officer + 60 O.R. 11th S.W.B. + 1 Officer 11th S.W.B., 2 Officers 4th Batt C.E.P. + 100 O.R. 4th Batt C.E.P. at I3 central sheet 36. Emptying cable water Bogade. Signed [signature]	

WAR DIARY or INTELLIGENCE SUMMARY

(Erase heading not required.)

11TH SERVICE BATT
NOV 1 1917
STH. WALES BORDERERS

Army Form C. 2118.

Place	Date	Hour	Summary of Events and Information	Remarks and references to Appendices
LAUNDRIES H5A 5 7 Sheet 36	6/10/17		Night working party of 2 Officers + 60 O.R. 1/1st S.W.B. + 2 Officers + 100 O.R. 4th C.E.P. Work dumping cable in I3D sheet 36. Party moonish returned from dump.	
	7/10/17	abt 11 am	a hostile plane dropped bombs in the vicinity of the 1/1st S.W.B. bivouacking one man being slightly wounded. Night party of 2 Officers + 60 O.R. 1/1st S.W.B. + 2 Officers 100 O.R. 4th C.E.P. Work dumping cable in I3D sheet 36 under Brigade Signal Officer. Colonel Partridge proceeded to U.K. on leave. Major O'Kelly assumed command of the battalion.	
	8/10/17		L.G. teams 1st S.W.B. relieved L.G. teams 10th S.W.B. in the front line during the morning relief complete 5.30 am. 1st S.W.B. relieved Coys L.G.s relieved 10th S.W.B. in the front line after dark. Relief complete 10.20 pm	
L' EPINETTE SUB-SECTOR ARMENTIERES SECTION	9/10/17		a quiet day on the 1st line of our patrols were in No Mans Land during the night. One of these patrols was fired on by hostile L.G. & M.G. but suffered no casualties.	
	10/10/17		a quiet day. One of front in No Mans Land during the night. no hostile patrols were encountered.	

WAR DIARY or INTELLIGENCE SUMMARY

Army Form C. 2118.

(Stamp: 11TH SERVICE BATT. NOV 1 1917 STH WALES BORDERERS)

Place	Date	Hour	Summary of Events and Information	Remarks and references to Appendices
L'EPINETTE SUB SECTION ARMENTIERES SECTION	11/10/17		Great truck and aircraft activity during the day plus 30 Hun aeroplanes over. None of our patrols were in NO MANS LAND during the night. One patrol under 2/Lt Ricks attempted to enter enemy front line but cut its way through enemy wire but failed to enter but were effort made to cut a gap. The last are 6 tanks	
	12/10/17		A quiet day. Hostile trench mortar & artillery activity was depressed. 2 of our patrols were in NO MANS LAND during the night. Major Hodgson went off duty sick. 5th army School of Musketry & Lewis gunners. 2nd Lieut Sgt def officer.	
	13/10/17		A very quiet day. No hostility of any sort reported. One of our patrols in NO MANS LAND during the night.	
	14/10/17		Slight increase in hostile artillery activity & marked increase in hostile aerial activity. Two Coys 11 S.W.B. relieved two Coys 11 S.W.B. in the front line these two coming back to the Subsidiary line Relief complete 10.15 pm. Major Digby proceeded to 115 Brigade H Qrs.	
	15/10/17		Slight increase on hostile trench mortar fire. lively activity very marked. 6 Huns tutting cutting wire & lamp during the day in front of the enemy distant line between D1A 70.20 & 15.D.30.65.	

WAR DIARY
or
INTELLIGENCE SUMMARY.

(Erase heading not required.)

Army Form C. 2118.

11TH SERVICE BATT.
STH. WALES BORDERERS
NOV 1 1917

Place	Date	Hour	Summary of Events and Information	Remarks and references to Appendices
LERINETTE SUB SECTOR ARMENTIERS SECTION	16/10/17		[illegible handwritten entries]	
	17/10/17		[illegible handwritten entries]	
LAUNDRIES H52 57	[illegible]		[illegible handwritten entries]	
	19/10/17		[illegible handwritten entries]	
	20/10/17		[illegible handwritten entries]	

WAR DIARY
or
INTELLIGENCE SUMMARY.

(Erase heading not required.)

Place	Date	Hour	Summary of Events and Information	Remarks and references to Appendices
LAUNDRIES H.5A.5-7 Sheet 36	21/10/17		One Major M.C. Coy Comm Major & Laundries from Eukenhangery for 24 hrs rest & W.O. One officer & 5.O.O.R D Coy 1st Batt. C.E.P 1st party arrived from Eukenhangery Calls in 15D under Brigade Signal Officer. A & B Coys worked in Front line by 2 Coys 10th S.W.B. A & B coys proceeded to LAUNDRIES & from 115 Bn pm Section for training	
	22/10/17		One officer D Coy 11th S.W.B returned to Sitewerbery & new relation by C Coy 11th S.W.B Came down to LAUNDRIES for 24 hrs rest & a bath. One officer & 5.O.O.R D Coy 1st Batt C.E.P proceeded at night to dump carts under Brigade Engineer Officer in I.5D about 36	
	23/10/17		One Hutton C Coy returned to Sitewerbery like & 1 Platoon of D Coy came down to LAUNDRIES for 24 hrs rest & a bath	
	24/10/17 25/10/17 26/10/17		Two A & B Coys training of 115 Brigade School & C & D Coys in ordinary trench under the command of O.C. 10 S.W.B	

Instructions regarding War Diaries and Intelligence Summaries are contained in F. S. Regs., Part II. and the Staff Manual respectively. Title pages will be prepared in manuscript.

WAR DIARY
or
INTELLIGENCE SUMMARY.
(Erase heading not required.)

Army Form C. 2118.

Place	Date	Hour	Summary of Events and Information	Remarks and references to Appendices
L'EPINETTE SUB SECTOR ARMENTIERES SECTION	27/10/17		Batt H.Qrs 11th S.W.B. relieved [illegible] 10th S.W.B. in the front line. Relief complete 12 noon. Dispositions were :-	
			Left Coy: D Coy 11th S.W.B. — Centre Coy: B Coy 10th S.W.B. — Right Coy: B Coy 11th S.W.B.	
			Reserve Coy: A Coy 10th S.W.B.	
			Subsidiary line — Left Coy: C Coy 10th S.W.B. — Right Coy: D Coy 11th S.W.B.	
			O.C. 11th S.W.B. assumed command of sub-sector at noon. Two patrols in No Mans Land during the night. The patrol of 2/Lt Lacey was surprised by large enemy patrol lying in a derelict trench. After an exchange of bombs our patrol was forced to retire 2/Lt Lacey being wounded.	
	28/10/17		Heavies, 18 pdrs & medium trench mortars fired on enemy front & support line between I.11.a.50.90 & I.5.d.10.50. Two patrols in No Mans Land during the night. One patrol reconnoitring enemy wire was heavily bombed & fired on by M.G. but sustained no casualties.	

A7092 Wt. W128 9/M1293 750,000. 1/17. D. D & L. Ltd. Forms/C2118/14.

WAR DIARY or INTELLIGENCE SUMMARY

(Erase heading not required.)

Army Form C. 2118.

Place	Date	Hour	Summary of Events and Information	Remarks and references to Appendices
LEPINETTE SUB SECTOR PROVENTIERE SECTION	30/9/17		Hostile artillery principally active on points B.8.a 50.30 + 4.5.D.0.50 + 4.5.D.1.15 enemy aeroplanes B.B. A.50.30 + 4.5.D.0.50 + 5.D.1.65 flew over the sector. The weather was fine and clear. At 6.30 p.m. 6 of the enemy aircraft came over, one of them shot down near the front line. Patrols & listening posts sent out as usual. Enemy observed to be very busy throughout the day. Wire entanglements remain plenty. Warning about [illegible] from more [illegible] [illegible]	
	30/9/17		We fired artillery on the enemy's front line 1 S.B.D. 4.5 + 1.5 C.9.2. The 18 lbs fired 220 rounds 15" 65.25.m. and 40.50 rounds. The medium trench mortars fired 5 rounds. 28 flares fired by M.G.'s and trench guns. The following activity during the day was reported. Our front line was quiet, with rifle fire.	

11TH SERVICE B[ATTALION]
NOV 1 1917
STH WALES BORDERERS

Army Form C. 2118.

WAR DIARY
or
INTELLIGENCE SUMMARY.
(Erase heading not required.)

Instructions regarding War Diaries and Intelligence Summaries are contained in F.S. Regs., Part II. and the Staff Manual respectively. Title pages will be prepared in manuscript.

Place	Date	Hour	Summary of Events and Information	Remarks and references to Appendices
LEPINETTE SDG SECTOR ARMENTIERES SECTION	1/11/17		Hostile artillery active. Heavies 18 pdrs + medium trench mortars fired on enemy wire between 15c 60 05 + 11 a 40 40. One of our patrols in No Mans Land during the night. Weather fine throughout the morning, snowing 12 noon.	
	2/11/17		Hostile artillery + trench mortars active. Heavies + medium trench mortars + light enemy wire between 15 c 60 05 + 11a 40 40 from 10am until it was too dark to observe. No Mans Land during the night, other enemy parties encountered, began to form ration parties during the night. Enemy patrol encountered in No Mans Land patrol was driven off with casualties. WEATHER stormy all the morning with storm during the afternoon & night.	
	3/11/17		Enemy artillery active during the day. Heavies shot on M.G. emplacement during the afternoon. Medium trench mortar fired on enemy wire between 15c 60 05 + 11a 40 40 between 2-4pm. Two patrols of ours in No Mans Land during the night. WEATHER fine in morning, cloudy in afternoon.	

22.V 8 sheet

Army Form C. 2118.

WAR DIARY
or
INTELLIGENCE SUMMARY.
(Erase heading not required.)

Instructions regarding War Diaries and Intelligence Summaries are contained in F. S. Regs., Part II. and the Staff Manual respectively. Title pages will be prepared in manuscript.

Place	Date	Hour	Summary of Events and Information	Remarks and references to Appendices
L'EPINETTE SUB SECTOR. ARMENTIÈRES SECTION	4/11/17		Head Quarters 10th Battn. S.W.B. relieved H.Qrs. 11th S.W.B. in the front line. Relief complete 2.55 p.m. Command of the sub sector passing to O.C. 10th S.W.B. at 3 p.m. WEATHER fine sunny day. 10.30 p.m. enemy shelled the sub. sector with lethal gas shells. Though the bombardment was heavy, only three men became casualties, kind slightly gassed. H.Qrs. 11th S.W.B. proceeded to billets in LAUNDRIES at H5a5.7.	shut 36.
LAUNDRIES H5A5-7.	5/11/17		A Coy 11th S.W.B. relieved B Coy 11th S.W.B. in the front line at dusk. C Coy 11th S.W.B. coming back into reserve. WEATHER cloudy.	
	6/11/17		D Coy 10th S.W.B. relieved B Coy 11th S.W.B. in the front line at dusk. B Coy coming back into subsidising line. WEATHER wet.	
	7/11/17		At 1.24 a.m. a raid of 10 Officers + 270 O.R. was carried out by 10th S.W.B. on enemy front + support line between [5c87.20 & I11a 35.32 shut 38. At 1.24 a.m. our artillery opened on enemy front line + afterwards lifted to support line + then formed a box barrage around raiders. The enemy wire was thoroughly cut + the raiders entered enemy front line + support lines. Two dugouts were blown up by R.E.'s. 14 prisoners were taken + it is estimated that at least 50 of the enemy were killed. WEATHER wet all day but stopped raining at night. Ten men per Coy 11th S.W.B. came from line to LAUNDRIES for 24 hrs rest & clean up.	

Army Form C. 2118.

WAR DIARY
or
INTELLIGENCE SUMMARY.

(Erase heading not required.)

Instructions regarding War Diaries and Intelligence Summaries are contained in F. S. Regs., Part II. and the Staff Manual respectively. Title pages will be prepared in manuscript.

Place	Date	Hour	Summary of Events and Information	Remarks and references to Appendices
Laundries A15.5.5.1	8/11/19		Sen men per coy at Laundries for rest returned to the line. Weather — Fine	
	9/11/19		Weather cloudy	
	10/11/19		10th Batt SWB relieved 11th Batt SWB in the front line. Two Coys & D 11th SWB proceeded to 115th Infantry Brigade School at Laundries for training & two Coys C & B 11th SWB proceeded to billets in Laundries. Weather — wet all day	
	11/11/19		The battalion spent the day cleaning up & re-equipping. A draft of 120 O.R. joined the battalion ex 3rd SWB Gt Britain. Weather — wet all day.	
	12/11/19		C & D training under 115 Infantry Brigade School & C & B Coys training under Batt arrangements. 110 O.R. & 1 Off. from C & B Coys on working parties during the day & night in the line carrying cables & carrying concrete. Weather — fine & sunny.	
	13/11/19		C & D training under 115 Infantry Brigade School. A & B Coys training under Batt arrangement during the morning. Recreational training in the afternoon (including football & boxing). 110 O.R. & 1 Off. from B coy on working parties during the day & night in the line bringing cable & carrying concrete. Weather — fine & sunny.	

Army Form C. 2118.

WAR DIARY
or
INTELLIGENCE SUMMARY.
(Erase heading not required.)

Instructions regarding War Diaries and Intelligence Summaries are contained in F. S. Regs., Part II. and the Staff Manual respectively. Title pages will be prepared in manuscript.

Place	Date	Hour	Summary of Events and Information	Remarks and references to Appendices
LAUNDRIES H5A5.7.	14/11/17		Presentation of two Distinguished Service Certificates to Cpl Rogers + Pte Evans of D.Coy for gallantry in connection with the capture of two Germans on the morning of the 20th Sept Oct 1917. C+D Coys continued training under 115 Infantry Brigade School arrangements. A + B Coys under Battalion arrangements. Lt Colonel Morgan proceeded on leave, majority of P O'Kelly assumed command of the battalion. Major C.D.P.Killijo to to second in command vice Major J. H.J. Monteith to to second in command of 115 Infantry Brigade School. WEATHER fine + sunny. 116 O.R. +1 Officer on working parties in the line, during the 24 hrs, besides work keeping cable + camping concert.	
	15/11/17		WEATHER fine + sunny.	
	16/11/17		11th S.W.B. relieved 10th S.W.B. less L.G. teams in the front line, relief complete 9.50.hm. L.G. teams 11th S.W.B. relieved L.G. teams 10th S.W.B. at very great night. WEATHER fine but cloudy.	

WAR DIARY or INTELLIGENCE SUMMARY.

Place	Date	Hour	Summary of Events and Information	Remarks and references to Appendices
L'EPINETTE SUB SECTOR ARMENTIERES SECTION	17/11/17		L G teams 11th S.W.B relieved L G teams 10th S.W.B at dawn relief complete 11.5 a.m. The T.Ms cooperated with the artillery in an organised shoot during the afternoon on the enemy front line trench & wire. Three of our Patrols in NO MANS LAND during the night but no enemy were encountered. WEATHER fine but cloudy.	
	18/11/17		Enemy artillery & trench mortar activity slightly on the increase but caused no damage. At 6.30 p.m. the enemy put up a very large number of different colored lights but no action followed. Three of our patrols in NO MANS LAND during the night. WEATHER fine but cloudy.	
	19/11/17		At about 5.35 am an enemy patrol was spotted our L.G opened fire wounding 4 of them, who were brought back in by a patrol that immediately went after them. The enemy then shelled our front at 15 & 5 50 very heavily all day both with artillery & T.M's also intermittent fire on the same front throughout the night. Three of our patrols were in NO MANS LAND during the night as enemy patrols encountered. WEATHER fine but cloudy.	

Army Form C. 2118.

WAR DIARY
or
INTELLIGENCE SUMMARY.
(Erase heading not required.)

Instructions regarding War Diaries and Intelligence Summaries are contained in F. S. Regs., Part II. and the Staff Manual respectively. Title pages will be prepared in manuscript.

Place	Date	Hour	Summary of Events and Information	Remarks and references to Appendices
LA FRIVETTE SUB SECTOR ARMENTIERES SECTION.	28/11/19		Heavy hostile shelling of our front line + support line especially at 15A4.5.50 + 11b6.50.90 about 36. This shelling caused 4 casualties. 1 killed + 3 wounded. Enemy artillery less active during the night. Weather fine but cloudy. Three of our patrols in No Mans Land during the night.	
	29/11/19		Heavy hostile shelling of our front line + support line by guns of calibres. T.Ms especially at 15A4.5.50 + 11b6.50.90. By moving very & our T.Ms to a flank we again escaped with very little damage only sustaining 1 casualty. Three of our patrols in NoMans Land during the night. No enemy encountered. Enemy T.Ms were active during the day. No retaliation. Weather fine rain all day.	
	30/11/19		10th S.W.B. [illegible] Ottens relieved 11th S.W.B. less 2 coys. Coys in the line relief being complete about 9.30 pm. 11 S.W.B - less 2 coys came back to SUBSIDIARY LINE. A + D Coys to [illegible] support and one Pln "C" Coy at AD.S. being in left subsector. (04-41/45 frm committees of 2 officers + 40 OR approved that PACK and L.G ammunition left by 11/RWF & found to be above C.O.Qy	

Army Form C. 2118.

WAR DIARY
or
INTELLIGENCE SUMMARY.
(Erase heading not required.)

Instructions regarding War Diaries and Intelligence Summaries are contained in F.S. Regs., Part II. and the Staff Manual respectively. Title pages will be prepared in manuscript.

Place	Date	Hour	Summary of Events and Information	Remarks and references to Appendices
LEPINETTE SUB SECTOR	22/11/17		H Batt. H Qr. moved back & billets at H36 c.7 about 3.6. WEATHER fine but cloudy with occasional rain	
ARMENTIÈRES SECTION				
SUBSIDIARY LINE	23/11/17		At 5.45 a.m. an enemy patrol was observed from No.1 Post. One of the enemy was observed to approach the post. When near L.G. reached. After dark this being was brought in. The rest of the patrol when warned retired with L.G. fire. Lewis guns of the 10th S.W.B. which was gone up to the L.H.S. were fired at. Enemy seen running movement approaching this type in the subsidiary line. WEATHER cold & showery	
ARMENTIÈRES SECTION	24/11/17		Shelling between 5 a.m. enemy of several about and 5 outward in support lines I5 a.7 C.29. Suffered heavily. Hostile TM's M9, M9. Co-operating. Enemy rifles was seen approaching our front line & opened out. Our casualties were 2 O.R. killed, & 2 Offrs. wounded, no Officer & 15 wounds. WEATHER fine but cloudy	
	26/11/17		Enemy artillery TM's much less active than previous days. WEATHER glassy with very heavy gale of wind.	
	29/11/17		A few heavy shells were fired into ARMENTIÈRES during the day, otherwise the situation was quiet. WEATHER stormy, with a high wind	

WAR DIARY
INTELLIGENCE SUMMARY
(Erase heading not required.)

Army Form C. 2118.

Place	Date	Hour	Summary of Events and Information	Remarks and references to Appendices
SUBSIDIARY LINE ARMENTIERES SECTION	27/11/17		A very quiet day. One Battle aeroplane flew over ARMENTIERES at 3 pm & was engaged by our A.A.A. and shrouded. WEATHER Showery.	
	28/11/17		1/18 L.F. Breuluid 16th S.W.Bers L.F. & returned to the trenches 11.20am. Relief complete at 11.20am. Right Sub sector Sulsubury Line Centre "A" Coy. Disposition Trenches Regt "D" Coy Centre "A" Coy Left "B" Coy. Reserve "C" Coy. All 9th 11th S.W.Borders. Subsidiary Line Right "B" Coy. 17th R.W. Fusiliers Left "A" Coy 17th Fusiliers Capt Mc Richm to S.W.Borders against Major Flood in command our Major C.D. Rudolph to Line. Situation quiet. WEATHER. The trenches	
L'EPINETTE SUB-SECTOR ARMENTIERES SECTION	29/11/17		been very D/11 South Wales Borderers relieved by 9/10 S.W. Borderers at dawn. Relief completed at 12 noon. Hostile shelling & trench mortar activity during the day. Our Artillery and trench mortars retaliated with our fire. 7.12 a.m. Two of our machines 2 points intercepted on our front. WEATHER: rain & sleet and showery.	
	30/11/17		Wind of some shelling of MORMEMAERES, mainly on D B 11. Flank AV. Quality Street, DISTILLERY & Adelard tram & Leatin. Hostile aircraft active at Capt TH. Morgan from Leave returning to unit & 2nd R.R. released. Major E. G. de O'Reilly to 11½ St.L. F.R. L. WEATHER Snow & rain during the night. Clear to evening.	

Anthony Lin Colonel
Commanding 9th in S.W.B

WAR DIARY
or
INTELLIGENCE SUMMARY.

(Erase heading not required.)

Army Form C. 2118.

Place	Date	Hour	Summary of Events and Information	Remarks and references to Appendices
LEPINETTE SUB SECTOR ARMENTIERES SECTION	3/11/17		Fourth month without casualties. Enemy fire 18 shots to medium trench mortars and 2 heavies, 75 of 5.9", 65 of 77, 80 of 4.2" and 60 of 10cm. Own fire on enemy area D.R.S.W.O. entries & on enemy front. ARMENTIERES was heavily shelled during the night with gas.	

[signature] Major

Commanding 11 J.W.B [?]

1-11-17

Army Form C. 2118.

WAR DIARY
or
INTELLIGENCE SUMMARY.
(Erase heading not required.)

Instructions regarding War Diaries and Intelligence Summaries are contained in F. S. Regs., Part II. and the Staff Manual respectively. Title pages will be prepared in manuscript.

Vol 23

Place	Date	Hour	Summary of Events and Information	Remarks and references to Appendices
L'EPINETTE SUB-SECTOR ARMENTIERES SECTION	1/12/17		[illegible handwritten entries regarding Armentieres, shelling, trenches, weather]	
	2/12/17		Between 9 a.m. & 10 a.m., 2 p.m. & 5 p.m. several shells & heavy trench mortar shells fell in ARMENTIERES & MOULINS. At 9 a.m. 12 h.m. & 3 p.m. shells fell in STANKE mine craters. Point Ballot. LA BLUE FARM. I.17.d. Sh. 36 NW.4. WEATHER. Fine & cloudy, rain during the day.	
	3/12/17		[illegible handwritten entries] ARMENTIERES ... 1.20 am 8 shrapnel shells fell near Mc.M.3 M.14.29.4.1.3. STAUKET ARMENTIERES ... WEATHER Fine and sunny.	
	9/12/17		[illegible handwritten entries] L'EPINETTE SUB-SECTOR ARMENTIERES SECTION ... WEATHER ...	

A. M. Chumley

Army Form C.2118.

WAR DIARY or INTELLIGENCE SUMMARY

Army Form C. 2118.

Place	Date	Hour	Summary of Events and Information	Remarks and references to Appendices
LAUNDRIES H5a 5.7	5/12/17	12 NOON	Lewis Guns 10th SWB relieved Lewis Guns 11th SWB in the front line, relief being complete at 12 NOON. Lewis Guns of "C" + "D" Coys front Temporary garrison of the SUBSIDIARY LINE & made L.G's 17th R.W.F. to relieve L.Gs 16th WELSH in front line left sub-sector. L.G's 11th SWB returned to reserve billets at the LAUNDRY H5a 5.7 after being relieved by L.Gs 15th WELSH. "A"+"B" Coys training under 115 Bde School. "C"+"D" Coys Working Parties & training. 4 Officers + 84 O/R's as guides + to work with Portuguese Working Parties. 10ffr + 1 as O/R's of total working under R.E. supervision + billeted in the SUBSIDIARY LINE. WEATHER fine.	
	6/12/17		"A"+"B" Coys at 115 Bde School. Working parties as 5/12/17. During the afternoon 12 hostile balloons drawn over lines & dropped pamphlets including "GAZETTE DES ARDENNES". WEATHER fine.	
	7/12/17		3 Officers + 76 O/R's as guides + to work with Portuguese. A+B Coys at 115 Bde School. WEATHER fine. Rain towards evening.	
	8/12/17		LT.COL. T.H. MORGAN proceeded for a course with R.F.C. Capt. I.A. MORGAN assumed Temporary command of the Battln. A+B Coys at 115 Bde School Working Parties as 7.12.17	
	9/12/17		Church parade in morning. D+B Coys at 115 Bde School Working parties as 7.12.17. WEATHER fine all day.	
	10/12/17		Lewis Guns 11th SWB relieved Lewis Guns 10th SWB in front line, relief being complete at 9 P.M. 1 Officer + 8 O/R's as guides + to work with Portuguese Working party. 11th SWB also L.G sections relieved 10th SWB also L.G sections in the Right sub sector. Subsidiary line Right S. Coy front line relief being complete at 10.30 P.M. Dispositions front line Right S. Coy	

WAR DIARY
INTELLIGENCE SUMMARY.
(Erase heading not required.)

Army Form C. 2118.

Place	Date	Hour	Summary of Events and Information	Remarks and references to Appendices
L'EPINETTE SUB-SECTOR ARMENTIERES SECTION	10/12/17 (cont)		Left "A" Coy. Centre "D" Coy. Reserve "B" Coy. Old of the 11th S.W.B. Subsidiary line. Right:- "A" Coy. Left:- Coy. both of the 10th H. S.W.B. WEATHER. Fine.	
	11/12/17		Enemy shelled back areas at 6AM & 11.30AM otherwise his Artillery was very quiet. He retaliated to our TM shoot with about 30 rounds on WILLOW Ave. Two of our patrols were out. WEATHER - DULL & MISTY - observation difficult. Two of our patrols were in NO MAN'S LAND during the night.	
	12/12/17		Enemy shelling battery positions most of the day. HV + TM's were fired between Nos H + 5 Posts + between Nos 1 + 2 posts. The day was generally quiet. Our aircraft very active 10 of our planes flying over our lines at 11AM. An enemy plane fell in flames about FREELINGHAM. Two of our patrols were in NO MAN'S LAND during the night.	
	13/12/17		A quiet day. [...] side. [...] returned [...] [...] Capt J.A Morgan resuming [...] [...] N. [...] has been more active during [...] [...] WEATHER mainly [...]	
	14/12/17		At 12-30 am a hostile patrol of 1 NCO + 2 O.R. attempted to penetrate [...] We were holding our front line. The party was challenged by [...] Hours of day frost with darkness at 2 O.R. wounded [...]	

WAR DIARY or INTELLIGENCE SUMMARY

Army Form C. 2118.

Place	Date	Hour	Summary of Events and Information	Remarks and references to Appendices
L'EPINETTE SUB SECTOR ARMENTIERES SECTION.	14/12/17		Patrols in our hands. Hostile artillery registered Heavy T.M. Kly on our W/Coy front. Two of our Patrols in NO MAN'S LAND during the night. WEATHER cloudy.	
	15/12/17		At 5.30 am a hostile raiding party of 1 Officer & 20 O.R. attempted to silently raid one of our posts. The night being very dark the enemy were unobserved until they reached the covered wire men immediately opened fire but only 5 of the enemy effecting an entry into our post. Sgt Brice attacked these with great dash & putting the enemy to flight leaving in our hands one prisoner whom Sgt Brice had knocked senseless. We sustained no casualties.	
	16/12/17		The Battalion was relieved in the front line by the 10th Battalion London Scots. Bordens. Battalion HQ. moving back to support at ARMENTIERES and the four companies moving back to the Subsidiary Line, dispositions from left to right being B. A. C. companies. Relief was complete at 11.15 pm. Lewis Guns were relieved earlier in the day.	
	17/12/17		Quiet day. Weather frosty and cold. Visited by Photographer & Representative of the "Western Mail" and "Newport Argus" & Post.	

WAR DIARY
or
INTELLIGENCE SUMMARY.

(Erase heading not required.)

Army Form C. 2118.

Place	Date	Hour	Summary of Events and Information	Remarks and references to Appendices
ARMENTIERES SECTOR	18/10/17		Personnel of Transport, Q.M. Stores and Battalion Head quarters fires in Lange of 38th Divisional Sniping Company. Orders received for relief of Battalion by 33rd Battalion Australian Prov: Force, and following party sent to SAILLY time reconnoitre by Officers and N.C.O's of 33rd Bn. A.I.F. 33rd Batt. A.I.F. relieved 11th S.W.B. in the SUBSIDIARY LINE, relief complete at A+B Coys proceeded to billets in BAC ST MAUR, C+D Coys + Batt H Qrs proceeded to billets in SAILLY SUR-LA-LYS. MAJOR MONTEITH returned to the Batt ex 115 Infantry Brigade School M. WEATHER very cold + dry.	
SAILLY SUR LA LYS	19/10/17		Cleaning up + resifting with inspections by Coy Officers. Veterans Coy Commanders reconnoitred defences of Bridgeheads across the LYS. WEATHER very cold + frosty.	
	20/10/17		Section + individual training throughout the day on fields allotted to the Batt. WEATHER very cold + frosty.	

WAR DIARY
or
INTELLIGENCE SUMMARY.

Army Form C. 2118.

Place	Date	Hour	Summary of Events and Information	Remarks and references to Appendices
SAILLY Sur la LYS	21/9/17		Section + authorised training throughout the day. The names appended in Sir Douglas Haig's dispatch of Nov 7. 1917. as "names deserving Special mention" Temporary Major J. H. S. Monteith " " Captain W. J. Harris 20048 C.Q.M. Sgt W H Golightly 22452 " " " F. Brun + the Corps Commander has awarded the Military Medal to Sgt F. Brun for his most excellent + brave conduct on the morning of the 15/12/17 in repelling an enemy raid on one of our posts. At 9 pm a Test alarm was given. The whole Battalion were in position with Transport camped in 60 mins. WEATHER cold + frosty.	
	22/10/17		Battn at Bn Baths in SAILLY for the whole day. A Military Medal was awarded to 31614 Cpl H. Evans for excellent work performed in capturing one of the enemy on the night 14/15 Dec 17. Lieut Colonel A. H. Radice our Commanding Officer who was wounded on 21/7/17 on the STEENBEEK was mentioned in Sir Douglas Haig's dispatch	

WAR DIARY
or
INTELLIGENCE SUMMARY.

Army Form C. 2118.

Place	Date	Hour	Summary of Events and Information	Remarks and references to Appendices
SAILLY SUR LA LYS	22/12/17		of Nov 7, 1917 and a name deserving special mention." WEATHER fine but milder, 35° & 40°.	
	23/12/17		11th S.W.B. proceeded at 8am to various parts of the SAILLY Bridgeheads to which of the assessment & defences to push a permit were present to which of the assessment of the general 3000 yds of often front was held but with some of the the following ment attending Sir Douglas Haigs talk of 1917 1917 and a name deserving special mention. Lieut Colonel F. Hodgson. WEATHER cold + frosty.	
	24/12/17		6th S.W.B. proceeded at 8am to continue cleaning. The whole task was finished a matter of about 3000 yds. WEATHER cold + frosty.	
	25/12/17		Church parade at 11.30. Men dinners at 1 o'clock when every had roast beef, turkey, vegetables, xmas pudding cigarette, apples, nuts & auditors when full at 5.30. WEATHER cold with showers of sleet	

WAR DIARY
or
INTELLIGENCE SUMMARY.

Army Form C. 2118.

(Erase heading not required.)

Place	Date	Hour	Summary of Events and Information	Remarks and references to Appendices
SAILLY SUR LA LYS	26/12/17		Training all day. There was breakfast a good deal by the heavy & warm storm during the night & also in showers the morning	
	27/12/17		WEATHER cold with snow during night & early part of morning. A & B Coys training at BAC ST MAUR. C & D Coys watching the first scheme of wiring in front of Bridgeheads of SAILLY.	
			WEATHER cold with light falls of snow	
	28/12/17		A. B. & C Coys training. D Coy wiring according to defence scheme.	
			WEATHER cold with light falls of snow.	
	29/12/17		A, B & D Coys training. C Coy wiring according to defence scheme. Inspection of C Coy by Commanding Officer. WEATHER cold with gentle thaw towards night.	

WAR DIARY
or
INTELLIGENCE SUMMARY.

Army Form C. 2118.

Place	Date	Hour	Summary of Events and Information	Remarks and references to Appendices
SAILLY SUR LA LYS	30/12/17		Church parade for A, B + C Coys. D Coy completed morning according to scheme. WEATHER slightly warmer to gentle thaw continuing	
	31/12/17		Whole battalion having a large portion of their training as recruits devoted to Musketry. WEATHER cold & dry	
	1/1/18		Training as above. WEATHER cold & dry.	

Lieut. Colonel
Comdg 11th (S) Batt. South Wales Borderers.

Army Form C. 2118.

WAR DIARY
or
INTELLIGENCE SUMMARY.
(Erase heading not required.)

Place	Date	Hour	Summary of Events and Information	Remarks and references to Appendices
SAILLY SUR LYS	1/1/18		Whole Batt training by Coy. WEATHER cold + dry.	
	2/1/18		Coy training continued. WEATHER cold + dry.	
	3/1/18		Coy training continued. The following appeared in the London Gazette Supplement 1/1/18. Awards for distinguished Service in the Field. Distinguished Service Order — Lt Col A. H. Rennie. Military Cross — 2/Lt M. W. H. Lancaster.	
	4/1/18		WEATHER slightly warmer with rain. Coy training continued. WEATHER cold + dry.	
	5/1/18		Coy training during the morning. Inter coy football matches + recreational training in the afternoon. WEATHER cold + dry.	

Army Form C. 2118.

WAR DIARY
or
INTELLIGENCE SUMMARY.
(Erase heading not required.)

Place	Date	Hour	Summary of Events and Information	Remarks and references to Appendices
SAILLY SUR LA LYS	6/1/18		Church parade. The following names appear in the London Gazette Supplement dated 1.1.18. 15249 R.S.M. W. Davies Distinguished Conduct Medal. 22075 Sgt A Giles " " WEATHER cold + dry.	
	7/1/18		Coy training for whole batt. The following name appeared in the London Gazette Supplement dated 1.1.18. 18734 Sgt G. Frost Distinguished Conduct Medal. WEATHER cold with heavy fall of snow.	
	8/1/18		Coy training for whole batt. WEATHER cold + dry.	
	9/1/18		Coy training for whole batt. WEATHER warmer, thawing rapidly	

Army Form C. 2118.

WAR DIARY
or
INTELLIGENCE SUMMARY.
(Erase heading not required.)

Instructions regarding War Diaries and Intelligence Summaries are contained in F. S. Regs., Part II. and the Staff Manual respectively. Title pages will be prepared in manuscript.

Place	Date	Hour	Summary of Events and Information	Remarks and references to Appendices
SAILLY SUR LA LYS	10/1/18		Coy training as before. A & B Coys commenced stretching 2 30 yds rifle range in factory B&C St Maor. WEATHER warm	
	11/1/18		Coy training as before. The 30 yds range completed. WEATHER warm & dry.	
	12/1/18		Coy training during the morning. Various officers of 12th Division reconnoitred the SAILLY BRIDGEHEADS. Weather warm & dry.	
	13/1/18		11th S.W.B. were relieved by 7th Batt East Surrey Regiment. Relief complete 1.50 p.m. 11th S.W.B. marched to billets at L 32 a & 7 sheet 36, the latter reported all in billets at 4.55 p.m. WEATHER colder & dry	
ESTAIRES AREA (SOUTH)	14/1/18		Coy training. O.C. Coys reconnoitre the crossings of the river LAWE. WEATHER cold with heavy fall of snow.	

Army Form C. 2118.

WAR DIARY
or
INTELLIGENCE SUMMARY.
(Erase heading not required.)

Instructions regarding War Diaries and Intelligence Summaries are contained in F. S. Regs., Part II. and the Staff Manual respectively. Title pages will be prepared in manuscript.

Place	Date	Hour	Summary of Events and Information	Remarks and references to Appendices
ESTAIRES AREA (SOUTH)	15/1/18		Training impossible owing to very heavy rain. 16 Officers + 11 N.C.O³ reconnoitre crossings of the LAWE.	Initials
	16/1/18		Coy training as far as the weather permitted. WEATHER wet.	Initials
	17/1/18		Coy training, C Coy firing on 30 yds min ature range until weather became too bad. WEATHER wet.	Initials
	18/1/18		Coy training, B + D Coys firing on 30 yds miniature range. Everything very wet, river LYS has overflowed its flood banks + flooded surrounding country + roads. WEATHER dry.	Initials
	19/1/18		Coy training. A + C Coys + A.Q. but fired on 30 yds miniature range. WEATHER warm + dry.	Initials
	20/1/18		Church parade for A, C + D Coys. B Coy + 30 O.R. from D Coy furnished working parties at L.28 b.90.90 + L.36 a. WEATHER warm + fine	Initials

WAR DIARY
INTELLIGENCE SUMMARY

Army Form C. 2118.

Place	Date	Hour	Summary of Events and Information	Remarks and references to Appendices
F. STAIRES AREA (SOUTH)	22/1/18		Coy training. Interplatoon Brigade Boxing competition in the evening. Cpl Brooker won his first contest with an opponent of 17th R.W.F. Lewis Coy musketry completion on 30 yds range. B Coy worm. WEATHER very warm.	
	23/1/18		Coy training. B Coy musketry team practicing on 30 yds range. WEATHER very warm.	
	24/1/18		Coy training. Brigade Cross Country run. We came in at [...] W.B. Coy Brigade team beat 17th R.W.F. Lewis Coy team. WEATHER warm.	
	25/1/18		Coy training. Coy practice 30 yd range. WEATHER warm.	
	26/1/18		Coy training. Bath recalled. Training in afternoon. WEATHER warm.	
	27/1/18		Whole batt working on rear defences. Digging strong points. WEATHER warm.	
	28/1/18		Whole batt working, digging strong points & connecting them together. WEATHER colder.	

WAR DIARY
or
INTELLIGENCE SUMMARY.

(Erase heading not required.)

Army Form C. 2118.

Place	Date	Hour	Summary of Events and Information	Remarks and references to Appendices
ESTAIRES AREA (SOUTH)	29/1/18		Batt working as previously. Weather cold.	
	30/1/18		Batt working on defences as previous. Weather cold.	
	31/1/18		Batt working on defences as previously. Weather very cold.	

Signed
Lieut Colonel
Comdg 11th (S) Bn S.W. Borderers

www.ingramcontent.com/pod-product-compliance
Lightning Source LLC
Chambersburg PA
CBHW081535160426
43191CB00011B/1763